that faith has an abiding story truer and deeper than even fear's deepest claims."

—Paul Andrews, member of the executive committee of
  Voices for a World Free of Nuclear Weapons

"The author suggests that if humanity stays on its present course, a nuclear war is inevitable. He urges policymakers and analysts to consider "what's next" after a nuclear war has been unleashed. He walks us through a religious take on the subject and comes to surprising conclusions. William Swing is uniquely qualified to discuss the nexus between religion and nuclear weapons, and he does so in a way that is fun to read, despite the pessimism that pervades the analysis."

—Ambassador James Goodby, foreign affairs specialist with the
  US Atomic Energy Commission's office in charge of the Nuclear
  Test Ban Treaty and former US ambassador to Finland

GOD and
NUCLEAR WEAPONS

Meditations at the
End of the Atomic Age

HOW NICE!
PEOPLE of
DIFFERENT
RELIGIONS
JOINING TO
WORSHIP
a HIGHER
POWER!

GOD and
NUCLEAR WEAPONS

Meditations at the
End of the Atomic Age

The Right Reverend
William E. Swing

Project Editor: Sandra Gary
Book and Cover Design: Barbara Geisler
Copy Editor: Maureen Perry

Drawing on title page courtesy of Signe Wilkinson
Photo on page 6 courtesy of Heide Betz
Photo on back cover courtesy of The Episcopal Diocese of California
Front cover photo by Pete Linforth from Pixabay

ISBN: 979 832 517 279 3
Library of Congress Control Number: 2024910004

All proceeds from the sale of *God and Nuclear Weapons* directly support the work of the United Religions Initiative.

Table of Contents

Dedicated to
Former Secretary of State, George Shultz,
who favored me with friendship in life's mix,
with companionship on our spiritual journeys, and
with leadership in the realm of disarmament.

Monica Willard, who vigorously promoted our
Nuclear Prayer and propelled it worldwide.

John Weiser, my closest collaborator on multiple
spiritual adventures. Without his support, this
book would never have been written.

My wife, Mary, always!

... let the whole world see and know that things which were cast down are being raised up, and things which had grown old are being made new, and that all things are being brought to their perfection by him through whom all things were made...

—THE BOOK OF COMMON PRAYER

Preface

In 2007, the late former Secretary of State George Shultz invited me to a round table seminar at the Hoover Institution at Stanford University on the topic of nuclear weapons. I was keenly aware of this privilege because experts in the field, from around the world, would be participating. I quickly accepted. When the two-day event began, I was positioned upstairs in the gallery where I took copious notes. Downstairs were those who had spent lifetimes addressing the entire range of issues related to nuclear weapons.

In the last moments of the seminar, George looked up into the balcony at me and asked, "Bill, what do you think?" I knew the words behind his words. What he was saying to me was this, "Bill, you have spent a lifetime studying sacred scriptures. You have preached thousands of sermons about God. Please step up and declare your deepest truth about this subject. We don't want a callow opinion; we are looking for your conviction. Perspective. Help us to go deeper!"

Though I did manage to conjure up a few thoughts at that daunting moment, his question has stayed with me over the years. George's challenge hit the center of my heart, and I have spent the rest of my life responding with actions, articles, and community building around the threat of nuclear weapons. This book is a much longer and more theologically considered answer to George's question, "Bill, what do you think?"

I am writing this book for three purposes. First, I want to pen a letter to George, posthumously updating the evolution in my thinking about nuclear weapons since 2007, including my thoughts on "the end of the world." Second, I want to challenge anyone reading this book to answer the same question, "What do you think?" What you think, if taken seriously, might just be the hope of the world. The world needs and deserves your answer. And third, I want it to be known that George Shultz was not only an economist, businessman, diplomat, and statesman, but also a man of abiding and inquisitive faith in God.

I addressed this latter point in the toast that I made to him on his 95th birthday when I said,

George once wrote, "I don't know how I got the way I am, but I am sure that my parents had a lot to do with it. They loved me, and I knew it."

His parents! His mother, Margaret Lennox Shultz, was the daughter of Episcopal missionary parents who died in Idaho. As a young girl, Margaret traveled to New York to live with an aunt and uncle, the Rev. and Mrs. George Pratt.

Meanwhile in the Midwest, a young farmer named Birl Earl Shultz won a scholarship, first to DePauw University and later to Columbia in New York City. Not only did he earn a PhD, but he won the hand of Margaret Lennox. And on this day, December 13, 1920, George Pratt Shultz was born to them.

From his mother's side of the family, George grew in faith. He developed a love of the *The Book of*

Common Prayer, and to this day, as the priest reads the service, George follows along closely 'because of the beauty and gravity of the words.' And today, when George arrives early to church, he picks up the hymnal and tries to understand the theology and piety behind the words. And ... from his mother, he inherited twin Menorahs which had been gifts to her family from the Jewish community in New York.

From the other side of his family, George admired the Quaker instincts of his father who could 'think quietly and talk gently about his views.' Although his father dreamed of becoming a university professor, he went to Wall Street to teach young people how the stock market worked. Many of George's aspirations were shaped by his father's move from university to practical application in the business world.

So, wherever George has gone in the world, he worshiped God, whether that was in St. Paul's Cathedral in London, where he would go and just sit. Or whether that was at a Seder in the United States Embassy in Moscow in Soviet days. Or in Tbilisi, Georgia, during the Cold War, surrounded by KGB guards. George, I am certain that your mother is proud of you.

When George arrived at Stanford in 1978, he was given a desk and a couple of chairs. No telephone. It was quiet. George said, 'I was working entirely from the inside out. I carried this wonderful habit ... through all the demanding jobs that I have had.' Trying to get down to the essence. George, I am certain that your father is proud of you.

George Pratt Shultz once wrote, "I don't know how I got the way I am, but I am sure that my parents had a lot to do with it. They loved me, and I knew it."

Blessings George, on your birthday!

In so many ways, George Shultz and I are opposites. He graduated from Princeton with honors. I was asked not to return to my college after two years. He fought in battle in the Pacific region during World War II. I watched World War II movies in my hometown. He earned a PhD in industrial economics from MIT and was dean of the Chicago School of Business. Four months after my ordination, the governing board of my church met to decide whether to fire me. He was the secretary of labor. I was sent to the smallest, dirtiest church (a plumbing garage with cross) in the diocese. He was the first director of the Office of Management and Budget. I had a little congregation in a pottery town. He was the secretary of the treasury. I started a church in a racetrack for the jockeys and hot walkers. He was secretary of state in Washington, DC. I became the rector of a parish in Washington, DC. Finally, we had something in common.

Later, In California, I was the bishop of the diocese of California and George was a parishioner at St. Bede's Episcopal Church in the diocese. We infrequently saw each other from a distance, until he began seeing Charlotte Maillard Swig, my dear friend and co-conspirator on numerous civic projects in San Francisco. George's wife, Obie, had died, and Charlotte's husband, Mel, had died, and eventually, I performed the marriage of George and Charlotte.

After that, George and I became buddies. When I was

housing 1,600 homeless people a night, George would come by. If he had a golf tournament, he would invite me to be his partner. If I gave a lecture at a Jesuit university, George would sit in the first row. If Henry Kissinger or Shimon Peres or Michael Bloomberg were visiting George, I was included. When I asked George to be an honorary trustee of the United Religions Initiative, he didn't hesitate. Nor did he when I asked him to help me start Voices for a World Free of Nuclear Weapons. Countless collaborations followed in multiple directions.

One day, Charlotte Shultz was in the hospital with a dangerous cancer. She said to me, "My mother had a solid religious faith. She took great comfort and strength from it. But I don't have that. And at this stage of life, I would like to begin a deeper journey into faith. Bill, can you help me?" I promised that I would create a Rule of Life for her with daily devotional practices. George was in the room and piped up, "I want a Rule of Life for me, too." All of that led to praying together, worshipping together, and celebrating the sacrament together.

This book is my final tribute to George Shultz.

The friendship between the Shultzes and the Swings created several initiatives that will have consequences around the world for generations. Left to right: Mary Swing, William Swing, Charlotte Shultz, and George Shultz, in 2005.

Introduction

Dear George,

It is the summer of 2023, and two blockbuster movies have come out, one about the Barbie doll and one about nuclear scientist Robert Oppenheimer. I haven't yet seen this three-hour Oppenheimer *movie, but I can't wait to do so. My highest hope is that it will wake up the public, especially the young, to the nuclear threat that you knew so well. In my conversations with the first few youths who have seen the movie, I was disheartened. I asked, "What did you think?" They said things like, "Very intense ... excellent cinematography ... great acting ... terrific movie ... I liked it as much, maybe more, than* Barbie."*

Since you left us, Russia has invaded Ukraine causing a staggering loss of lives, suffering, displacement, and destruction. Now that the Russians are not going to win quickly, as they intended, Russia is talking about using tactical nuclear weapons on Ukraine. They have even moved such weapons to Belarus, and Alexander Lukashenko, the president of Belarus, has voiced his readiness to use these weapons on Ukraine. Despite all of this, "In the first four weeks since its release in Ukraine, the movie, Barbie, *has grossed slightly more than three million dollars, making it the highest grossing movie ever released by Warner Brothers in Ukraine," according to "News From Ukraine" by Chomiak and Homans in Graham Seibert's online newsletter of August 18, 2023. No mention of the* Oppenheimer *movie. I guess if my next-door neighbor had nukes and talked about dropping them on me, I too might choose* Barbie *over* Oppenheimer *for entertainment.*

In this summer of 2023, I want to focus on Oppenheimer, himself, at the beginning of this book for two reasons. First, because his use of the word "Trinity" gives me a way forward in outlining this book. Second, and more important, he gives poetic, ultimate weight to the word "resurrection." That an atomic scientist would evoke a religious term when facing the prospect of becoming "the destroyer of the world," I find to be a deeply prescient assertion.

"The Atomic Age" was ushered in with a project whose code name was Trinity.

"Trinity?" Why "Trinity?" No one knows, but generally it has been accepted that J. Robert Oppenheimer, Director of the Los Alamos Laboratory, chose the word. If so, what was Oppenheimer thinking?

Over many years Oppenheimer provided several hints, thus giving the impression that his answer evolved. Early on, he quoted from John Donne's 1623 "Hymn to God, My God, in My Sickness" writing, "As West and East, on all flat maps—I am one—are one. So death doth touch Resurrection."

John Donne drew a straight line from predictable death to the surprise of resurrection, and J. Robert Oppenheimer followed that straight line. This book will follow that same line from the predictability of nuclear holocaust to the unpredictability of the world's resurrection.

On another occasion, Oppenheimer quoted from John Donne's devotional poem, "Holy Sonnet 14," "Batter my heart, three-person'd God." This isn't conclusive evidence that his Trinity was fashioned after the Trinitarian doctrinal thinking of Christians, but it does suggest, at least, familiarity.

J. Robert Oppenheimer was a well-read man, careful in his calculations and conversant with religious texts of various traditions. So why did he reach into his lexicon and pull out a very Christian sounding word such as "Trinity" to speak in code about the first weapon of mass destruction? Was he thinking poetically, theologically, mathematically?

Or perhaps "Trinity" was a Hindu reference. Might he have been thinking of Brahma the creator, Vishnu the preserver, and Shiva the destroyer?

Or was he perhaps thinking about the three fundamental particles that make up the atom: protons, neutrons, and electrons?

Oppenheimer had witnessed four devastating years of war, knew of the Holocaust, read about the atrocities at Nanjing, was keenly aware of the total brutality and slaughter in those places. In his mind, he was certainly resolute that it had to come to an end. And just maybe the bomb—his bomb—could do that. Clearly, he was determined to succeed before the Germans did. The end was in sight and hiding under the code word of "Trinity." And Oppenheimer succeeded!

Afterwards, he quoted a verse from a Hindu holy book, the Bhagavad Gita (XI, 12), that says, "If the radiance of a thousand suns were to burst once into the sky, that would be like the splendor of the mighty one." In the bomb, could Oppenheimer duplicate the radiance of suns, perhaps?

Many years later (as reported on the atomicarchive.com website), he said that running through his head at the time of the explosion were these words, "We knew that the world would not be the same. A few people laughed; a few people cried. Most people were silent. I remembered the line from the Hindu scriptures, the Bhagavad Gita, Vishnu is trying to persuade the prince that he should do his duty and, to impress him, take on his multi-armed form and say, 'Now I am become Death, the destroyer of worlds.' I suppose we all thought that, one way or another."

The mystery of the code word "Trinity" remains. Code words transmit messages of brevity and secrecy. It is no longer a mystery as to what "Trinity" meant in terms of creating the world's first atomic weapon. What we are left to wonder about is what "Trinity" meant to Oppenheimer and why he used it. Trinity River, nearby? Trinity Mountains, nearby? Christian Trinity? Hindu Trinity? A Trinity of Physics? And what does his "Trinity" mean to us who inherit his legacy of a world armed with nuclear weapons?

I, as an eighty-seven-year-old man, who lived ten years without the weapons and seventy-seven years with the weapons, have my own perspective. Yes, I am a Christian clergyman and an interfaith leader, thus my deepest perspectives are inspired in the context of myths, prophecies, theology, and religious history.

My "Trinity" regarding nuclear weapons in 2023 consists of: The Choice, The Nightmare, and The Hope.

PART ONE

THE CHOICE

During wartime bombings, there is always collateral damage. So, when the choice is made to drop bombs, the extent of devastation is unknown at that moment. Only much later is the magnitude of a despoiled earth and the extent of human carnage discovered. The choice to create nuclear bombs, prepare for nuclear war, and ready nuclear bombs for instantaneous release, presents the possibility of incalculable loss in collateral damage. Where it ends is a mystery.

But where it starts is with a choice.

CHAPTER 1

Hiroshima and the Garden of Eden

On August 6, 1945, President Harry Truman was returning from a trip to Europe when he announced, "The world will note that the first atomic bomb was dropped on Hiroshima, a military base." He went on to say the bomb harnessed, "the basic force from which the sun draws its power … it is an entirely new force in the universe." Then the news commentator at WNBC New York replied, "The power to control it is the biggest query as to the world's future." Wryly, the next piece of music played on that radio station was sung by the Ink Spots, "You always hurt the one you love, the one you shouldn't hurt at all."

The first two critical choices had been made. Scientists had chosen to pursue and harness "the basic force from which the sun draws its power," while the political leaders had chosen to unleash "an entirely new force in the universe." This picture lifts human endeavor to an almost divine or mythic level. We now clutch, in our hands, power that had been reserved for the sun or for God. Thereafter, our ultimate choice, along with the world's future, hinges on our "power to control it." Our 1945 choice in Hiroshima is updated to the 2023 choices in Ukraine and beyond.

To respond to that challenge today, as use of tactical nuclear weapons threaten Ukraine, I suggest that the biblical story of the Garden of Eden gives us a fascinating perspective on the anatomy of choices where the world's future hangs in the balance. To assist us in broadening our ultimate context, we might take a moment to make a moral journey from our nuclear-armed "locked and loaded" warheads and take a walk through the Garden of Eden filled with delicious as well as forbidden fruit. See if anything in the story speaks to our nuclear reality of the 21st century.

Spoiler alert: the choice that Adam and Eve made meant the end of their world. And to be fair, it is only a myth. Nevertheless, while a myth will not tell us what is historically true, it sometimes has the power to show us what is true about history.

In the garden, God supplied Adam and Eve with ample fruit of rich varieties; everything that they would ever want. But with a warning: in the middle of the garden was one tree … whose fruit they were forbidden to eat. God said, "If you eat that fruit, you will die."

As Adam and Eve were staring at that forbidden fruit, clearly fascinated and tempted, Satan in the form of a snake said, "You will not die … you will be like God." Obviously, they had a choice to make, just like the creators and the decision-makers of the atom bomb did. Just like the choice that we must make today! We are still "like God" and we hope that we won't die.

From the first announcement of the bomb's debut, the overwhelming fear has been that we will die. All of us. The world with all its life forms will die. If we go from the garden to Hiroshima, if we go from the forbidden fruit to nuclear weapons, we might find some parallels.

"You will not die … you will be like God," said the serpent. Seventy-eight years have come and gone since President Truman's announcement, and life on earth hasn't died, even though we have chosen to take on the godly role of building ever more powerful bombs and watching eight other countries, both friends and enemies, do the same. The nine nuclear-armed nations are: the United States, Russia, the United Kingdom, France, China, India, Pakistan, North Korea, and Israel. Maybe the old snake was right. The forbidden could be digested, and life's equilibrium would not be damaged.

Mikhail Gorbachev and Ronald Reagan, two former farm-country boys who became presidents of their respective countries, met in Geneva, Switzerland, in 1985, and agreed that the plethora of nuclear weapons in the world was insane, and that something catastrophic was bound to happen. They didn't believe the snake in the garden—that they were like God and that no one would die. So, they declared, "A nuclear war cannot be won and must never be fought." Thus began the long, arduous road toward reducing the number of warheads, expanding strategic conversations, and binding treaties.

Nevertheless, the promise of the old snake in the grass prevails today. For 4.5 billion years, planet Earth did not have nuclear weapons. Floods, yes! Plagues, wars, meteor hits, yes. Nevertheless, we muddled through without nuclear weapons, and the earth supplied our basic needs. Now, in the past seventy-eight years, we have lived with our nuclear weapons. So, 4.5 billion years without nukes; seventy-eight years with nukes. To our credit, not one such bomb has been dropped on an enemy since 1945. And the number of nuclear warheads has been reduced from about 70,000 to about 13,000 today. That's the good news.

As for the bad news, there is lots of it. Presidents of the

United States have contemplated using nuclear weapons and considered alarming choices. President Eisenhower thought about using nuclear bombs on Korea. President Richard Nixon actually ordered their use in Viet Nam, according to an article by Laicie Heeley published by the Outrider Foundation in 2019. Heeley wrote, "After a US spy plane was downed in North Korea over the Sea of Japan, killing thirty-one Americans, George Carver, the CIA's top Vietnam specialist at that time, recalls that Nixon became incensed and ordered a tactical nuclear strike. Henry Kissinger and the joint chiefs agreed to do nothing until Nixon sobered up in the morning." A drunken president ordering a nuclear weapons attack! Absurd! Presidents can make disastrous decisions about nuclear weapons.

Atomic bombs have dropped from our own airplanes by mistake and landed in North Carolina and South Carolina. One Russian colonel "saved the world" by not unleashing the Russian arsenal on the United States. He simply didn't trust the data he was presented. Also, we lived through the earth-endangering stand-off of the Cuban Missile Crisis of 1962. Simple dumb luck and wise choices have been our resources as we have charted our way through "The Atomic Age" thus far.

In the garden, the snake promised that we could do that which was forbidden, and we would not die. Well, going from myth to the real world, we haven't died from harnessing "the basic force from which the sun draws its power." So far so good; but the world sleeps nervously.

The other prediction, that we would be "like God" seems to have some truth to it. Haven't we developed the internet and the web, and aren't we on the doorstep of an artificial intelligence (AI) future? Vastly expanded human discoveries seem almost infinite. But along comes the danger. "AI tools and technologies, they're relatively cheap," said Rob Reich, Chancellor's Professor of Public Policy at University of California, Berkeley, in the *San Francisco Chronicle* of March 30, 2023. They are "often available in open access, open-source modes, it's akin to saying at the beginning of the nuclear age, what would it be like if everyone could play with plutonium and uranium?" Like God?

Dear George,

One of my profound regrets was not interviewing you more fully about the time when you and Gorbachev and Reagan were in Reykjavik, Iceland. I am sure that "who said what to whom" has been carefully chronicled. I would like to know what it felt like, what were the vibes when you all imagined cutting the number of warheads from 70,000 to a smaller number. And then, what was in the air when you all looked squarely at the prospect of eliminating all nuclear weapons (the world's last great moment of hope). I know about the stumbling block of "Star Wars" and the difficulty of selling these ideas "back home." But I don't know the level of inward excitement—beyond all of the hard negotiations—when the future of the planet was on the table. Perhaps that moment called for such earnest calculations and dueling agendas that feelings had to take a back seat. Nevertheless, did your heart skip a beat, ever, in Reykjavik?

WHAT DO YOU THINK? Now that we Americans have succumbed to the temptation to have nuclear weapons, what have we gained, and what have we lost? Are we better off now with these weapons? How so?

CHAPTER 2

The One Who Makes the Choice

On the ceiling of the Sistine Chapel is Michelangelo's scene of the finger of God stretched out touching the finger of Adam at the beginning of Creation. Five centuries after Michelangelo, our reality is that the finger of our representative Adam, the president of the United States, is poised above the nuclear trigger that could bring about the end of Creation. The touch of one finger determines everything.

Once a human finger has touched the finger of God and the fate of the earth has been bequeathed to that one, how does that one keep his/her finger off the nuclear button? Up to now in the United States of America, we have had an answer to that question. Adam, our representative person, alone has the power. Adam, a.k.a. the president, can either choose to launch the nuclear holocaust or refrain from doing so. None of us has a vote in the matter.

What's wrong with this picture? Every major religion in the world realizes the blasphemy of this scene. But no faith has a vote. The ultimate decision lies in the political sphere. Whichever political party wins the election has its own designated Adam placed in position to end civilization. The absurdity of nuclear weapons with a human finger on the trigger causes some of us to work for the reduction and final elimination of nuclear weapons. Despite these efforts, matters now seem to get worse. Instead, the nine Adams of the nine nuclear-armed nations have ever more devastating weapons created while little "wannabe" Adams gather fissile materials hoping for their day on the ceiling of the Sistine Chapel. They have sole authority without having soul authority.

In the church that I am part of, The Episcopal Church, each Sunday we can pray together for the president of the United States, whether that person is Republican or Democrat. I don't have a vote in these matters, but I do have a prayer. And moral outrage!

I joined with Tyler Wigg-Stevenson, who is the author of *The World is Not Ours to Save*, to write an article on "The Shame and Horror of Nuclear Weapons." We zeroed in on the president at that time, Barack Obama. Here are excerpts from that article that appeared in the August 6, 2015, issue of *The Week*.

The newly inaugurated President Obama described his nuclear policy vision in Prague on Palm Sunday in 2009. He stated, "As the only nuclear power to have used a nuclear weapon, the United States has a moral responsibility to act … So today, I state clearly and with conviction America's commitment to seek the peace and security of a world without nuclear weapons."

This line—and the ambitious disarmament and nonproliferation agenda that the speech laid out—are arguably what won President Obama that year's Nobel Peace Prize. Six years later, however, his bold declaration of nuclear abolition seemed less prophetic than the throat-clearing caveat that immediately followed when he said, "I'm not naïve. This goal will not be reached quickly—perhaps not in my lifetime."

The power of nuclear weapons is such that we instinctively scrabble at theological language to describe it. The terrible consequence of such linguistic grasping, however, is that we come to treat the bomb as an implacable god or force of nature over which we have no control, and then we bow before the work of our own hands in the manner of idolatry.

This is why Obama's caveats are so devastating and, in hindsight, unsurprising. When he took the podium in Prague, there was no one on earth who had more power over the fate of nuclear weapons. But in one rhetorical stroke—"perhaps not in my lifetime"—he granted nuclear weapons functional immortality. In fairness, too, a hostile Congress on one side and an aggressive Russia on the other have curtailed further incremental progress.

Could a Nobel Peace Prize be returned?

In hindsight, the president's actual nuclear policy, in action since Prague, is commendable. His administration has pursued a series of strategic moves, foretold in the Prague speech, which reduced Cold War bloat, secured nuclear materials against terrorism, and enhanced nonproliferation.

The moral courage regarding nuclear weapons that President Obama promised—but has failed to deliver—is not just a transcendent ideal, but also a pragmatic imperative. These are weapons whose singular quality is their exponential multiplication of the human capacity for destruction. If we, their makers, fail to rid the world of them, then our bombs and ourselves will one day fly away together.

Regardless of the names of the nine nuclear-powered heads of state, all of them (and sometimes their advisors), are genuinely mythical characters. With their nukes, they step out of the world of myth into reality and have Earth as their ultimate target. They are likes gods and have their fingers hovering over the buttons of destiny.

Dear George,
You have advised several presidents of the United States and you have negotiated with several leaders of other countries. Did you notice a certain nuclear hubris in the attitudes of the nuclear-armed presidents? Or was there recognizable moral heaviness in their conversation about these weapons?

WHAT DO YOU THINK? Decisions to use nuclear weapons lie in the purview of presidents. Can you think of a wise counselor for a president in these matters? What are some of the considerations that deserve to be pondered by a president before launching the weapons?

CHAPTER 3

The Real World

The existence of nukes poses many problematic issues. For instance, isn't the world too big to fail? And, haven't we, in the past, been inventive enough to think our way out of every peril that we have faced? And didn't we drop a bomb on Hiroshima and end a war, thus bringing peace to the world? If the bomb could bring peace in the past, why couldn't it do the same in the future? More bombs, more peace!

No one wants to destroy the natural order of this planet, but now that we have the weapons to do just that, how do we make choices to keep the bombs and the planet? When Nikki Haley was the United States ambassador to the United Nations, in 2017 she told CNN, "There is nothing I want more for my family than a world free of nuclear weapons. But … we have to be realistic."

Ah, realists! Who will prove to be the real realists when the bombs leave the silos and submarines and airplanes? On their way down to the ground, maybe the military-industrial complex folks who produce the bombs with the backing of the politicians and the voters, maybe they will turn out to be naïve idealists. Because they believed that the weapons, in the right hands, would save Earth. On the other hand, maybe the actual realists will turn out to be the cartoon characters with long beards carrying signs saying, "The End is Near."

What is real at this moment is that our US submarines can launch 400 nuclear weapons in fifteen minutes—fifteen minutes—and destroy every large city in Russia. "Real!" Just imagine a Russian missile called "Satan II" carrying the most warheads ever assembled on a missile, and they are aimed at us in America. When the final missiles are fired, words like realist and idealist will not matter. No words or anything will matter, because we will all be consumed in the hot essence of real evil itself. For what greater evil can there be than to destroy life on earth? If the most heinous world leaders and heinous regimes, in all history—Hitler, Stalin, the Khmer Rouge, the Spanish colonialists, and on and on—if their crimes against humanity were added together, they would be infinitesimally tiny compared to the crimes that we are planning to execute in a few moments.

In the meantime, we, nuclear-armed human beings, are doing the best, the best that we know how, now that we have nuclear know-how. For instance, since 1968, 191 nations, through the Treaty on the Non-Proliferation of Nuclear Weapons, have agreed to bring about "complete disarmament under strict and effective control." In my opinion, that is the world's highest statement of accord. Also, there is the International Campaign to Abolish Nuclear Weapons, as well as the failsafe strategy of the Nuclear Threat Initiative ... plus, the myriad doctors, scientists, students, jailed activists, and countless others who have devoted their lives to the abolition of nuclear weapons. Their "hair is on fire" with moral passion. A multitude of serious people whom the world labels as "idealists," but I see as "realists."

On the other side, I have the utmost admiration for all sorts of people who have made a commitment to safeguard these weapons. For instance, I am thinking of a particular naval officer aboard a nuclear-armed submarine whose job it is to perfectly—I mean perfectly—keep the weapons secure and to make certain that nothing goes wrong, all the while on supreme firing alert. I thank God for him and the others like him who provide the world with the best disciplined, diligent safeguards imaginable. I could add diplomats, scientists, physicians, and others to that list.

Once, I had the opportunity of having lunch with the head of the Joint Chiefs of Staff. In the flow of conversation around the table, someone asked the honored guest, "Could you think of any scenario in which the United States would ever use a nuclear weapon?" He thought about the question quietly for some time. Then he said, "No, I cannot imagine our country ever using a nuclear weapon." That statement left me pondering whether it's true. If it is true, and we will never use these bombs, then why build them, and modernize them? Just to have a stand-off of monumental proportions?

Regardless of our most conscientious efforts, at the end of the day, just before the bombs go off, we are still left with impossible choices: We must choose the bomb or grandchildren ... the bomb or springtime ... the bomb or music ... radiation or creation!

I can think of three choices for achieving a world free of nuclear weapons. 1) Let's drop the bombs on everyone, even drop them on ourselves. When there are no longer people, then there will be no more nuclear bombs. Perhaps, a few animals would have a chance of living in that kind of nuclear-free world. 2) The nine nations armed with nuclear weapons can come together and figure out ways to dismantle the nukes before it is too late. Note: this kind of thing has been done before when there were only two armed nations. 3) Keep going on our present course of proliferation among an expanding number of countries with the weapons, and when total annihilation of all life comes, then trust in the Author of Life to inaugurate life in a new dimension, a dimension without nuclear weapons.

Dear George,
What astounds me is that, regardless of the near misses and the dumb luck, the fact that Pakistan has not used the bombs, the fact that North Korea has not used the bombs—and the others—seems almost unbelievable to me. The safeguarding systems of all the nuclear-armed nations have kept the world safe, up to now. Given the monumental threat, all involved have diligently kept the weapons in harness. On the one hand, I say, "Thank God." On the other hand, given human nature, I am certain that this restrained trigger will not hold over the long run. I say, "Lord have mercy."

WHAT DO YOU THINK? Once "the genie is out of the bottle," once we learn to live with nuclear weapons, are we committed to go wherever the weapons take us? Are the weapons themselves the final decision makers? And, if we are saving the weapons for just the right moment, what might that moment be?

CHAPTER 4

God and Religion

Dear George,

I owe you profound gratitude for introducing me to the work of Andrei Sakharov. It was just a moment in passing for you but a stellar moment for me. I was in your office one day when you were surrounded by Russian experts and physicists, and you announced that the 25th anniversary of the death of Andrei Sakharov was approaching. Your idea was to have a two-day celebration of his life and work. Papers would be written and eventually printed in a book. All of this was far outside my knowledge zone, especially because I had no idea who Andrei Sakharov was. Then you turned to me and said, "Bill, I would like you to write the first paper."

I immediately said, "Yes, of course, George, I would be honored." In the next few minutes, I came to realize that Andrei Sakharov was a physicist. Perfect. I flunked first-year Physics in college three times, and the professor gave me a D-minus-minus to get me out of his class just before graduation. True. Terror drove me to research Andrei Sakharov for the next six months. I am glad that I did, because two aspects of his life have etched themselves on my memory and heart.

First was his Nobel Prize speech read by his wife, Elena Bonner Sakharov on December 11, 1975. He wrote, "It is unbearable to consider that at this very moment that we are gathered together in this hall on this festive occasion, hundreds and thousands of prisoners of conscience are suffering from undernourishment ... They shiver with cold, damp, and exhaustion in ill-lit dungeons, where they are forced to wage a ceaseless struggle for their human dignity and their conviction against the 'indoctrination machine,' in fact against the very destruction of their souls."

Sakharov paused his speech and took time to mention 114 prison internees, by name, prisoners known to him. By name in his Nobel speech! Then he said, "I should like all those whose names I have forgotten to mention to forgive me. Every single name mentioned as well as unmentioned, represents a hard and heroic human destiny." So said the man called "the father of the hydrogen bomb." He realized that the possessors of the weapons had lost their sense of humanity.

Second, as a devoted atheist, at the end of his life, Sakharov said, "I am unable to imagine the universe and human life without some guiding principle, without a source of spiritual 'warmth' that is nonmaterial and not bound by physical laws. Probably this sense of things could be called 'religion.'"

As a young man he said, "The physics of atomic and thermonuclear reaction is a genuine theoretician's paradise. A sun and stars, the sustenance of life on earth but also the potential instrument of its destruction—was within our grasp." So, he grasped. Like Adam and Eve, as well as you and me and all of us who live and die with the bombs we continue to perfect.

Dear George, it appears to me that for Oppenheimer and Sakharov, the world ultimately became a haunted house. The shadowy terror that frightened them now frightens us if we dare, for a minute, to open our eyes wide to see the true nuclear landscape that surrounds us. Living in a haunted house, our *second-best approach is to practice denial. The first and better approach is to shine light on the darkness and eliminate the agents of terror.*

GOD

Nuclear weapons and God inexorably go together. Why? Because they represent the final claims on the planet Earth. Nuclear weapons are bigger than the United States. Bigger than Russia. Too potent to be contained in a moment of time. Nuclear weapons represent the ultimate property dispute between God and Satan. The serpent might be saying to us, "In the old days, when you were innocent, God seemed to be the most powerful force on earth. But with the bomb in your hands, you are the most powerful force—whoever you are." Possession translates to dominion over all life on this planet. At the end of the day, nuclear weapons are a theological, not a military or political matter. "God might be the first word of life, but you can be the last word of death," the serpent might say. This is snake logic and perhaps our ultimate temptation.

It is as if Satan is trying to make a bet with God. God keeps saying, "If they keep this up, the entire human experiment will be terminated." However, Satan says, "They will not die. I'll wager you (pause), the earth." And God says, "It's a bet." And here we are in the middle of their contest.

Whose Earth is this planet? Does any nation own it, deserve riparian rights down to the shores of all its oceans? Who deserves homage at the bottom of all graves and the tops of all mountain and mushroom clouds? Is it all ours? At the last? Do we have the whole world in our hands?

A contemporary example of "snake logic" was reported by the *International Business Times* in their June 3, 2023, issue. Russian professor Sergey Karaganov was quoted as saying, "The creation of nuclear weapons was the result of divine intervention. God handed a weapon of Armageddon to humanity to remind those who had lost the fear of hell, that it exists." Keep in mind that this man was an advisor to Russian President Vladimir Putin. He went on to say, "Morally this is a terrible choice as we will use God's weapon ... but if we do not do this, not only Russia can die, but most likely the entire human civilization will cease to exist." To complete his tortured logic and theological madness, Karaganov talked about Russian launching "a preemptive retaliatory strike to counter any aggression."

With our weapons, we have lost our innocence. That is why, down deep, when we watch North Korea parading their nukes through their streets, we blush with shame at the entire enterprise. That is why drunks sitting at bars watching news about their political rivals, yell "Nuke 'em all," as if nuclear weapons were the final answer to life's seemingly intractable problems. We instinctively feel queasy as we tread on the sacredness of life with our nukes. In our bones we know that we are trafficking in blasphemy. We have gobbled up the forbidden fruit and are en route from the Garden of Eden to "the valley of the dry bones." Nukes have everything and nothing to do with God.

RELIGION

One might expect religion to be a strident foe of nuclear weapons since these weapons appear to make earthly creatures into gods, as the serpent advertised. Indeed, religions go on record in opposition to nukes. Almost every major religion in the world has written an anti-nuclear weapons statement. At the invitation of Pope Francis, I participated in the Holy See's Dicastery of Integral Human Development on November 10 and 11, 2017, and heard him give a ringing condemnation of every country for possessing nuclear weapons. Other religious leaders have issued similar statements. Nevertheless, when nationalism is part of the equation, religions can change their tunes.

For example, On May 3, 2019, Westminster Abbey hosted a service for the Royal Navy recognizing fifty years of the United Kingdom having nuclear deterrents at sea. The Dean of Westminster prayed that the Navy would never have to use the weapons, but added, "We give thanks for all the thousands of people who have designed, built, supported, and crewed the submarines." The Church of England walks a thin line between God, nukes, and nation.

In Russia, this connection between nuclear weapons and religion is even more pronounced. Patriarch Kirill unashamedly and enthusiastically blesses the country's nuclear weapons on behalf of the Russian Orthodox Church. Dina Adamski, in his book, *Russian Orthodoxy: Religion, Politics and Strategy*, writes about the "longstanding nexus between the Russian Orthodox Church and the country's nuclear-military-industrial complex." He states, "Russian nuclear orthodoxy constitutes the collective belief that to preserve its Orthodox character, Russia must be a nuclear power." Bomb and faith marry.

In my travels through Pakistan, I would hear people say with great pride, "India has a Hindu bomb, and now Pakistan has a Muslim bomb." There is something about these ultimate weapons that spills over into the territory of the Divine in the world of religions.

The one exception would be some Christians who await a moment of "Rapture," a moment when the entire world will explode in final conflagration, and they—the chosen—are carried into heaven while everyone else on earth writhes in the agonies of the end, all in the Name of Jesus. Nuclear holocaust is just fine with them. It is even welcomed!

Therefore, although most religions are officially on record as being fervently against nuclear weapons, they don't move beyond written pronouncement to take up advocacy and they seem to cave and avoid this subject altogether. Almost no sermons are preached from pulpits focusing on nuclear weapons. Almost no religious classes are held on nuclear weapons. Almost no prayers are uttered about nuclear weapons in houses of worship. Why not?

Perhaps what is going on is a case of collective denial. Folks in the pews don't want to hear about this, and the preachers don't want to depress the listeners in congregations. If religion is about the ultimate matters of life and death, it would seem reasonable that preachers would focus on life and death weapons. But no! Perhaps the bombs constitute the "dirty little family secret" that the families of faiths want to relegate to silence. Quiet because we know that we are part of something hideously obscene? Quiet because we are impotent in the face of an all-potent weapon? Quiet because we don't want to appear unpatriotic? Quiet because we don't care? Quiet because we want religion to make us happy?

A great many religious people in the United States go on a high-pitched harangue trying to deny women in distressed pregnancies the right to have an abortion. But when it comes to producing nuclear weapons that are aimed at annihilating hundreds of millions of babies and children, along with adults, those same religious people are silent. Religious nuclear silence!

Nuclear weapons are morally neutral. They don't have a mind or a soul. They don't make distinctions between religions or nationalities. They are now built not merely for victory. They are built for extinction—total extinction. Thus, they authentically launch us into the realm of the sacred and the demonic. We all eventually become like Andrei Sakharov, the designated "father of the hydrogen bomb." In the book *Andrei Sakharov: The Conscience of Humanity*, he said, "We scientists, engineers, craftsmen, had created a terrible weapon, the most terrible weapon in history, but its use would be entirely out of our control. The people at the top ... they would make the decision. Of course, I knew this already—I was not naïve. But understanding something in an abstract way is different from feeling it with your whole being, like the reality of life and death."

" ... Feeling it with your whole being, like the reality of life and death" is exactly what religious people in pulpits and pews do not want to feel. Instead, religions seem to have made their peace with deterrence.

Perhaps we simply trust that if we have nuclear weapons available on our religion's side, then we can deter any armed nuclear nation with religion on its side. This approach to deterrence has merit. As stated, we haven't had a nuclear weapon used in war for seventy-eight years.

But the trouble with deterrence is that it works until it doesn't work, and then it is too late. It works until Putin uses a tactical weapon in Ukraine. Deterrence works until we "modernize," and Russia "modernizes," and China "modernizes," and North Korea expands its reach and on and on, through time. Believing in deterrence, the world simply waits for the opening gambit of the closing of life on earth.

I think that deterrence is necessary as a temporary shield behind which the armed nations can strive to "bring about complete disarmament under strict and effective control," as the Non-Proliferation treaty puts it. On the other hand, if deterrence is a shield to hide behind in order to proliferate and modernize the weapons, then deterrence is only a fig leaf in the garden of naked exploitation. At best, deterrence is a time-limited necessity, not a long-range solution. If it lasts too long, then our vaporized life on earth will leave no legacy beyond a radioactive puddle!

WHAT DO YOU THINK? If religions tend to be tribal and nuclear weapons tend to be more universal, is this a mismatch? Aren't the weapons more important than the religions? Aren't religions subservient to and dependent upon the largesse of the nuclear-armed nations?

CHAPTER 5

Prayer

Dear George,

One of the great introductions you provided for me was to General James Mattis. Since then, we have carried on in-depth communications covering a wide range of issues. My highlight was when he and I spoke at Stanford in a conversation titled, "A Bishop and a General Discuss Peace." After the speech, I invited him to have dinner. He said that he would, but he had to drive all night (from the Bay Area to the state of Washington) to make a presentation to a gold-star family late the next morning. Since he was once an acolyte in a church in his home state, I keep telling him that it is not too late to channel his devotion to duty and become a priest. He only smiles.

In his book, *Rage*, author Bob Woodward describes a day when James Mattis, then secretary of defense, was with President Trump and other members of the national security team. They were going over the state of nuclear weapons in the world. When the meeting concluded, General Mattis got in a car, drove immediately to the National Cathedral, knelt in the Bethlehem Chapel, and prayed.

How human and how understandable! If someone has intimate and firsthand knowledge of the precarious fragility of the world because of the bombs, praying might be the one soul-led thing to do. If your eyes look directly at the bombs, you pray. At least, that is what General Mattis did.

In 2008, I went to see people who had seen what Mattis had seen. I went to former Secretary of State George Shultz, former Secretary of Defense William Perry, Ambassador Thomas Graham, national security specialist Sidney Drell, Ambassador James Goodby and a few others. Together we established Voices for a World Free of Nuclear Weapons (Voices). Our purpose was to be opportunistic about raising the issues of nuclear weapons and thus encourage others to take action toward the reduction and ultimate abolition of these weapons.

At our monthly meetings we started saying a prayer. We called it, "A Nuclear Prayer." It says,

> The beginning and end are in your hands,
> O Creator of the Universe. And in our hands,
> you have placed the fate of this planet.
>
> We, who are tested by having both creative
> and destructive power in our free will, turn to
> you in sober fear and in intoxicating hope.
>
> We ask for your guidance and to share in your
> imagination in our deliberations about the use of
> nuclear force.
>
> Help us to lift the fog of atomic darkness that
> hovers so pervasively over our Earth, Your Earth,
> so that soon all eyes may see life magnified by
> your pure light.
>
> Bless all of us who wait today for your Presence and
> who dedicate ourselves to achieve your intended

peace and rightful equilibrium on earth.

In the Name of all that is holy and all that is hoped.

Amen.

Every month, for the past fifteen years, we have begun each one of our meetings by reciting this prayer. Why? Our unspoken assumption is that as human beings, we are answerable to a higher Source regarding what we do with this beautiful planet which we have inherited. We are not nuclear slaves waiting for the orders of a nuclear-armed president. The issues at stake are far more profound than the Republican or Democratic parties or arms manufacturers or lobbyists or deterrence apologists. As human beings, we understand the gift of this good earth to be sacred and holy and to require us to be answerable to the entire enterprise of life on this planet—as it exists among the planets and stars in our galaxy. We intend our prayer to be a plea to the Originating Force of the Universe, to be a primal scream from Mother Earth to the Author of Life and to the common sense that is woven into the DNA of survival.

We made a video of all of us saying this prayer. Now, that prayer has a life of its own. Soon our prayer was said at many meetings of the United Nations. People around the world picked it up. It was translated into multiple languages. A group dancing in the Judean desert sang the prayer on video.

The destructive potential of these weapons touches a deep place in human hearts throughout the world. This is not surprising. When one opens one's soul to the real threat dangling over our heads, the visceral, automatic response is often, "Nuclear weapons … Oh, God!"

Toward the end of his life, Mikhail Gorbachev, former president of the Soviet Union, joined our little Voices group in inaugurating a Voices Youth Award. Gorbachev once wrote, "I believe in the cosmos. All of us are linked to the cosmos. So, nature is my god. To me, nature is sacred. Trees are my temples and forests are my cathedrals. Being one with nature." Personally, I consider this to be the prelude to Gorbachev's own Nuclear Prayer.

Prayer moves nuclear weapons from being a national security matter to being a primitive matter of the soul. There would never be such a weapon unless souls were not feeling threatened, fearful, vindictive, lusting for leverage and filled with pride. Deeply so! Why else would human beings embrace the potential of universal suicide? What kind of being would deliberately pursue annihilation for all life? It could be a human being whose soul was so blindly hurt and depraved as to create such weapons and then give endless rationales as to why the weapons make sense. Moral madness!

Why pray? First, when people all over the world join to raise their deepest concerns to their Highest Power, then hope and solidarity replace the feeling of nuclear helplessness. Second, such praying stops us from thinking that nine nuclear-powered heads of state are the final authorities of life on this planet. And finally, such praying sets us in search of leaders who will deliver us from nuclear self-destruction. A nuclear prayer from the depths of our souls is a bold action of hope as well as a prelude to Earth-saving actions that will be required of us.

I also wrote "A Child's Nuclear Prayer," which was not really for children but about children. Originally published in a Voices for a World Free of Nuclear Weapons newsletter in 2022, It goes like this:

> In St. Petersburg, Russia, a little girl kneels by her bed at night to say a prayer. In St. Petersburg, Florida, a little boy kneels by his bed to say a prayer. They use the same words, "Now I lay me down to sleep; I pray the Lord my soul to keep. If I should die before I wake, I pray the Lord my soul to take." What could possibly cause the death of a Russian child and an American child at night as they sleep? The answer hovers over their beds, in the dark, swirling around the world, and aimed at them. Nuclear weapons! The nightmare that promises that a child "could die before I wake."

The children will never see the weapons. The warheads are hiding in submarines underwater. Some are underground and unapproachable. But they are real. Practically invisible, but they are part of a secret and dark universe that has been created to destroy the world, if need be, in the name of national security. Almost unimaginable, nevertheless … imagine!

Imagine a nuclear torpedo designed to create a tsunami wave so high that it could contaminate an enemy's coastline cities with radiation for wide stretches.

Imagine 27,000 miles in space, there is a little satellite, the size of a school bus, which is a nuclear watchtower in the sky.

Imagine a general flying around in an airplane named "Looking Glass," armed with a "go-code" to launch all our nuclear weapons.

Imagine the president of the United States having minutes to decide whether to obliterate life as we have known it and then flying off in an airplane called "Doomsday."

We adults seem so childish, playing with such evil beyond any scale of morality or common sense. Someday it is possible that we will blow up the last children on earth. We are building weapons to do just that. Yes, the children in each St. Petersburg should pray.

Then again, maybe the two St. Petersburg children, today, will wake up praying, "Now, I rise to face this storm and fight for children yet unborn. May I awake before I die and banish nukes and clear the sky."

"The only people who should be allowed to govern countries with nuclear weapons are mothers, those who are still breast-feeding their babies," said Tsutomu Yamaguchi, the woman who is the only survivor of the Hiroshima and Nagasaki bombings.

Forced to live with the weapons dangling over our grandchildren, prayer is a legitimate choice for us.

Dear George,

I remember when we were filming our Nuclear Prayer in New York and at Stanford in 2012, and you came up with your own such prayer. Your prayer: "Dear God, Please bring common sense and Divine guidance to our work on the problems that nuclear weapons pose to our world. Man has invented a means to destroy us all. We must eliminate these weapons in order to preserve a sane and peaceful world. We pray for your help as we work toward this goal. Amen."

WHAT DO YOU THINK? If religions have not "cornered the market" on prayer and if all individuals can make their deepest appeal to an invisible Divine Mystery—more enduring, more powerful than our nukes—then can there be such a thing as a universal Nuclear Prayer? Without words? A soulful worldwide sigh of alarm and supplication? Has the presence of nuclear weapons changed the nature of prayer for you? Or in your soulful thinking, does prayer exist in one dimension while prayer exists in another, unrelated, dimension?

PART TWO

THE NIGHTMARE

Nuclear Weapons are deeply personal. They touch a place in the human soul where one has to wrestle with demons and angels. Are we basically good? Or bad? Are we engineered to destroy ourselves or create a beautifully advanced world? Am I responsible for the ultimate weapons and their consequences? Will our bottomless greed totally pollute the rivers of life? Instinctively, we know that these weapons represent a mirror in which we don't want to picture ourselves. A dream we don't want to entertain. A nightmare that holds our dread and keeps us from opening our eyes.

CHAPTER 6

Noah and the Flood—
Earth and the Nukes

A nightmare happens when one is asleep. Our brains take the ingredients of our experiences, fears and puzzles and rearrange them into a frightful scenario. And sometimes life itself presents us with a nightmare, not a bad dream, but a horrific reality. My guess is that nuclear weapons in 2023 reside in our unconsciousness as well as being a waking terror. How deep and how far back does the threat of everything being destroyed go? How present is the potential of a catastrophe beyond measure? That is what I want to explore.

I try to imagine being a child sitting around a fire 3,500 years ago, hearing the adults recite from memory the following tale:

> The Lord saw that the wickedness of humankind was great in the earth and that every inclination of the thoughts of their hearts was very evil continually. And the Lord was sorry that he made humankind on the earth, and it grieved [the Lord] to his heart. So, the Lord said, 'I will blot out from the earth the human beings that I have created ... I am sorry that I have made them.' But Noah found favor in the sight of the Lord. (Genesis 6: 5-8)

As a youngster listening around the fire, I imagine that I would have wondered: Are we really that bad? Is the Lord really that sad? What did Noah do to "find favor" in the eyes of the Lord? Primitive questions. And just maybe, my life, our lives today, hinge on the fundamental moral elements embedded in this story. That is why I will devote the next chapters to exploring possible modern answers to ancient, childlike questions—in the context of nuclear weapons.

Like the Garden of Eden, the Noah story is a myth. And while myths do not tell us what is historically true, sometimes they can shed light on what is true about history and humanity.

Destruction is only the first half of the Noah story. Yet it is enough to tell us that over 3,500 years ago, people realized that Earth is not too big to fail and that humans as a collective are not exempt from ultimate accountability and annihilation. Nevertheless, the Noah story unlocks the mystery of what is required to survive.

Dear George,

We are entering the part of this book that focuses on the short-comings, evil, misdeeds of us all. When these are on a personal level—"Thou shalt not steal … commit adultery … bear false witness" —that is one thing. They are occasions when we do harm to some other individual or betray our values.

It is entirely another thing when our cumulative malevolencies harm oceans and races and species and the global climate. We are accountable, according to the Noah story, for what we do collectively. "The wickedness of humankind was great in the earth."

In this 3,500-year-old myth, folks figured out that human

beings have moral accountability "in the earth." If they/we don't measure up to our stewardship responsibilities for the earth and to all of earth's peoples, then the earth will have no place for us. The world's mythical apocalypse in the Noah story is akin to the possible nuclear apocalypse of our own day.

Also, George, when the people in Noah's day looked up in the sky, they saw blue and thought it was water. Since rain (water) came down from the sky, it made sense to them. What held all the water in the sky back was something called "the firmament," which served as a gigantic barrier. If the firmament gave way, the earth had no chance. Today, we look into space and fear that our firmament, our Outer Space Treaty of October 10, 1967, doesn't hold, and the sky might fall down on us, not mythically but in reality.

As you well know that treaty bans the stationing of weapons of mass destruction in outer space, prohibits military activities on celestial bodies, and details legally binding rules governing the peaceful exploration and use of space. But, in 2023, there are at least 44,500 space objects circling Earth and many of them hold great military significance for wars on earth and portend wars in space. Someday, nuclear wars might be guided from space and take place in space.

WHAT DO YOU THINK? For you, does the Noah story of the flood have any parallels with our potential nuclear weapons story? If "the firmament" doesn't hold up in the myth, could the existing Outer Space Treaty not hold up in our real world? If the treaty breaks and the flood of bombs drop from the sky, will you have an ark? How would you build it? Who would ride in it with you?

CHAPTER 7

Are We Really That Bad?

George Bernard Shaw presented a blistering assessment of our fallenness in 1903 when he wrote a four-act play, "Man and Superman." In it, the devil has a soliloquy which could easily apply to today's nuclear weapons and the tendencies of us all. Keep in mind that this play was performed some 40 years before nuclear weapons, but its message carries current relevance.

The devil says,

There is nothing in Man's industrial machinery but his greed and sloth: his heart is in his weapons. This marvelous source of life of which you boast is a force of death. Man measures his strength by his destructiveness.

The highest form of literature is tragedy, a play in which everyone is murdered at the end. In the old chronicles you read of earthquakes and pestilence and are told that these showed the power and majesty of God and the littleness of Man. Nowadays the chronicles describe battles ... the greatness and the majesty of empires and the littleness of the vanquished. Over such battles the people run about the streets ... egg their governments on to spend hundreds of millions of money in the slaughter.

The power that governs the earth is not the power of life but of death and the inner need ... for a more efficient engine of destruction.

Shaw's nightmare echoes today in the "modernization" of nuclear weapons and the race to produce "more efficient engine(s) of destruction." Weapons have always evolved. So even though the nuclear weapons of today pose a dire life-altering threat, in another hundred years or so, human beings will come up with "advanced" weapons which will dwarf today's bombs.

The question that comes to mind is this: What kind of people are we that would put our ultimate trust in nuclear weapons? Have we been engineered this way from our birth? Or did we make ourselves into the highly weaponized beings that we have become? Do our weapons reflect our true nature?

Not long ago, I was in a meeting with people who are committed to the reduction and abolition of nuclear weapons. I noticed a young lady who didn't say a word. At the end of the meeting, I asked what she might be thinking. She said, "Young people my age don't think about nuclear weapons. We think about guns. Guns in school, in grocery stores, in churches, in concerts. Assault weapons built to massacre a great many children and adults. They are everywhere and protected by our laws. If our society cannot govern itself with sensible gun laws, what chance is there that we can govern ourselves with sensible approaches to nuclear weapons?" Are we really that bad?

Even when we try to do something to end a war, something like creating an atomic bomb, even then our toxicity keeps right on giving. Over a twelve-year period, we dropped atomic bombs on the Bikini Atoll twenty-three times. Consequently, all inhabitants had to be deported. Today, according to a story in the April 3, 2023, issue of the *New York Times*, "The golden sand of Bikini Atoll is laced with plutonium. The freshwater is poisoned with strontium. Coconut crabs contain hazardous levels of cesium."

Voices member Linda Cataldo Modica brought to my attention a plaque from New Mexico that reads, "The first victims of a nuclear bomb were American babies. The world's first atomic bomb exploded in New Mexico in 1945 at Trinity site. The Santa Rita Church in Carrizozo, New Mexico was forty miles from the blast and contains the names of the children who died that year. Ages 1 day to 1 and 1/2 years old. A 400 percent increase, from the last year (1944) in the death of children. Domingo Chavez, Dolores Sanchez, Juan Jiron, Maria Sedillo, Mary Lou Ortiz, Patricia Vega, Prescila Portillo, Sandra Jaurequi, Ramona Apodaca, Ramon Baca." Are they martyrs in the quest for national security? Or something else?

Germany tried to produce the cleanest energy possible, so it invested heavily in the nuclear variety. But after tragedies due to radiation released from power plants at Fukushima Japan in 2011 and Chernobyl Russia in 1986, Germany closed its last three nuclear energy plants. Now comes the problem: what to do with the deadly high-level radioactive waste which can remain deadly for hundreds of thousands of years? "Currently the waste is kept in interim storage next to the nuclear plants being decommissioned," said a CNN broadcaster in a story aired on April 15, 2023. "But the search is on to find a permanent location where the waste can be stored safely for a million years." A million years! We don't just bury our dead; we now must bury our toxicity for a million years. Are we really that bad?

Obviously, there is a great deal of difference between nuclear energy and nuclear weapons. Nuclear energy can provide clean power or can be used in nuclear medicine, whereas nuclear weapons have only one use and that is destruction. Nevertheless, they both end up with the same problem of disposability.

If Germany is looking for sites to bury its toxic waste and, if it looks to the United States for advice, it could be directed to solutions found here. What solutions? Bury all the really bad stuff on Native American lands. For instance, in 1855 the United States promised the Yakima Nation that it would have the right to hunt and fish on the land near Hanford, Washington. Today there are 54 million gallons of radioactive sludge buried there and might stay there forever, according to a New York Times story from June 1, 2023.

There is another possibility. Go to the Western Shoshone Nation in Nevada, to the Yucca Mountain and make that the depository for all our nation's nuclear waste. Wouldn't it be the saddest of ironies if this nation's founders got the land of America from the tribal people and in return, gave the tribal people toxic waste forever? What a legacy! Are we that bad?

Forever? If there were a nuclear war, what is the likelihood that all human life would be obliterated? In the *Bulletin of Atomic Scientists*, on October 22, 2022, François Diaz-Maurin, with the help of a number of scientists, provided an answer in his article, "Nowhere to Hide: How a Nuclear War Would Kill You—and Almost Everyone Else."

He calculated the human destruction of a regional nuclear war between Pakistan and India. Approximately 27 million would die in 24 hours. If a nuclear war broke out between the United States and Russia, he calculated that their 4,000 nuclear weapons of 100 kilotons would kill about 360 million within 24 hours. But other nuclear-armed countries would most likely get involved, as well, bringing about 1,200 nuclear warheads with them.

After that, greater damage would follow. Although the bombs would have severe consequences within a few days, the most profound damage to the environment and human life would inexorably follow over a few years.

"Two years after a nuclear war—large or small—famine alone could be more than ten times as deadly as the hundreds of bombs," says Diaz-Maurin.

In a very short time after an atomic war, nuclear weapons would become a climate issue. Using climate models, Diaz-Maurin figures that the devastation would start with radiation, then progress to heat, then a fireball of superheated air, then firestorms in cities leading to stratospheric soot injection, loss of our ozone layer, and years of "nuclear winter." Radioactive contamination would rain down for years. Lands and ocean would be dramatically compromised. Widespread famine would cause societal collapse. This collateral damage might result, two years after the nuclear war ends, in 5,341,000,000 deaths from famine.

Since there are over eight billion people on this planet in 2023, if we lost over five billion people to nuclear war and environmental calamity, then there still might be three billion people alive a couple of years after the end of our nuclear war. Cynically stated, "Therefore, there is a safety net under our proliferation of nuclear weapons." Only five billion dead! Thus, we can continue to proliferate the weapons, and life will go on. Are we that bad?

"Humans have made such a profound impact on our planet that our soot, plastics and radioactive fallout have been preserved in the earth. It has led geologists one step closer to formally naming an epoch: the Anthropocene Epoch or the age of humans. Scientists propose that the age of humans began in the 1950s with the nuclear age," said Suzanne Nuyen, reporting an NPR story that aired on July 16, 2023. The assumption might well be that this age ends with the bombs.

Finally, on this theme, the Budapest Memorandum deserves attention. On December 5, 1994, in Budapest, Hungary, an international coalition made security assurances to Ukraine, Belarus, and Kazakhstan. The memorandum called for these three countries to abandon their nuclear arsenals to Russia. In exchange, Russia, the United States and the United Kingdom agreed to: respect the independence and sovereignty of these countries with their existing borders; refrain from ever threatening or using nuclear weapons against these three countries; and other guarantees.

So, Ukraine, which had the third largest nuclear weapons arsenal in the world, gave its weapons to the Russians. At the time, Ukraine had physical but not operational control over the Soviet nuclear weapons. As for Russia's part of the bargain, in 2014, Russia made its move to take over the Ukrainian territory of Crimea. Then on February 24, 2022, Russia invaded Ukraine causing the greatest refugee crisis in Europe since World War II, bringing about the deaths of hundreds of thousands of Ukrainian men, women and children and destroying many cities. Plus, Russia has threatened to use tactical nuclear weapons against Ukraine. Are we really this bad?

Dear George,
It is hard for us humans not to taint whatever we touch and not always out of malicious intent. For instance, in a hymn of praise or a prayer of adoration we likely would use the word "God." One little three letter word! "God!" Nevertheless, isn't it slightly sacrilegious to use any one word in addressing the unspeakable, inexhaustible mystery of the Divine? Reducing the infinite, unfathomable to a small three letter word? Our language makes God smaller, small enough to fit into our language, our human experience, our limitedness. Our heart's intent is genuine, but our words are impossibly inadequate.

We are learning through space telescopes, artificial intelligence (AI), research labs, theoretical physicists, how utterly vast is this universe, at least the universe as we perceive it in the summer of 2023. To presume to speak to, to pray to, to sing to the Author and Sustainer of it all seems instinctive and natural to many people. But our language of praise is a work-in-progress.

Yet, we are only time bound, itinerant, and temporary beings looking at the larger picture of life and needing some language, however inadequate, to give voice to our deepest yearnings. It is commonly remarked that Muslims have ninety-nine names for God (actually, a lot more). Jews have names such as Adoni, Elohim, and Yahweh. Christians use the Divine Trinity: Father, Son and Holy Spirit. Our names don't exhaust but only hint at the object of our adoration.

Considering how many people have been killed, raped, and tortured in the Name of God, it seems incumbent upon all believers of all the God names to return to or adopt a prim-

itive humility. "We've all sinned and come short of the glory of God." (Romans 3:23) If there will ever be any degree of unity and respect among the faiths, it will have to include—perhaps begin with—an acknowledgement that our understanding the fullness of the Originating Divinity is far off. No one owns or has exclusive franchise rights to the name of God. We are all light years away from fully comprehending such Majesty. To end the worldwide fierce competition among religions, a competition which brings so much ignorance and suffering, the Name of God needs, first of all, to elicit universal humility and solidarity among us all in the quest for the Divine.

As to the question: are we this bad? In the realm of religiously motivated violence over the centuries and now, indeed, we are that bad. At the same time, even in our narrow-mindedness, there have been and are occasions where we have reached deeper mutual understanding and together, accomplish good things.

WHAT DO YOU THINK? Despite all the rotten things that we humans are capable of, we are nevertheless also originators of great beauty and kindness. We create stunning music and lasting art. We genuinely seek to heal and nurture others. We bravely explore unknowns. Therefore, all our good and bad—two by two—are gathered on this already-built ark called Earth. Perhaps the heavy weapons that we carry aboard will sink our ship. If we are already on the ark, fleeing the imminent destruction wrought by the weapons, what would prompt us to bring them on board?

CHAPTER 8

Is the Lord Really That Sad?

This section deals with "The Lord" as mentioned in Genesis 6:5-8. "The Lord saw the wickedness of humankind … " These words begin the first part of the Noah Story. Let's take a closer look.

First, it was an adult story. Today, the story of Noah and God is usually retold for children. An Ark, animals two by two, floating around; lots of jokes are made of this scene. But over 3,500 years ago, it was a serious story told by grown-ups to grown-ups who were trying to understand the big picture. Trying to figure out why people consistently take such harmful and destructive actions against others and against themselves. Trying to discern the mind of the Lord.

This myth emerged many centuries before Christianity or Islam. Much earlier, it was incorporated into the canon of the Hebrew scriptures. Also, several other flood myths circulated in other countries, for instance in the Gilgamesh Epic of Mesopotamia, circa 2100-1200 BCE. Ancient human beings created epic stories to make sense of life, just like we do. Some of the unique characteristics of the Noah epic are:

A MATTER OF THE HEART
What lies at the center of this story is the heart of humans and the heart of the Lord. For instance, the text reads, "The Lord

saw … that every inclination of the thoughts of their hearts were very evil continually." The Lord was not merely looking at their outward deeds but at their inward desires. There were no Ten Commandments to obey or disobey in this epic. The basic covenant between the Lord and humankind was a matter of the heart, both their hearts.

THE LORD HAS EMOTIONS

"And the Lord was sorry," the text reads, "it grieved [the Lord] to his heart." Evidently it was not so much about entering into judgment that caused the watery condemnation. Instead, it was basically that the heart of the Lord was broken because of the malfunctioning hearts of the humans. The story does not portray an angry God blindly striking out against wicked subjects. What the story does portray is a God of earth-shaking sorrow. This sorrow was the cauldron in which the death of all life was forged into a new chance for people to be fully human. The Lord made the rains drown every human and animal and creeping being, in sorrow.

"The Lord was sorry that he made humankind on the earth, and it grieved [the Lord] to his heart," the text reads. Failure! Not just human failure but Divine failure. The Lord and the people were in this together. The waters were the way to cleanse this entire situation of fallenness.

THE SURPRISE ENDING

"But Noah found favor in the sight of the Lord," the text reads. Wait a minute! Who was this Noah? Where did he come from? Was he a perfect person with no evil in his heart? As it turned out, he could faithfully take orders. He was a carpenter who could build an ark. The singular clue is that he "found favor in the sight of the Lord." But what did that mean? Why did the Lord favor Noah?

My wild guess is that the Lord saw sorrow in the being of Noah. Apocalyptic sorrow as if he realized that the human enterprise was about to be fated for extinction. The Lord and Noah shared the same ultimate sorrow.

Just as the Lord was sorry, perhaps Noah was the one person who came back with an antiphonal statement of grief. Everyone else just did what they do and were content with excuses and rationales. When global destruction is deserved and imminent, perhaps the only way out is to start with sorrow and build for tomorrow.

Maybe, just maybe, this is the key to the nuclear weapons crisis today whereby all life is getting close to drowning in radiation. All the politicians, strategists, members of the military-industrial lobby have their speeches down pat. "If we don't modernize the weapons, our enemies will, and thus have leverage over us," they say. "Our national security requires superiority of such weaponry," they say. "What is better than deterrence?" they say. As if the way things are now, is the ways things always will be.

What they don't understand is that the Noah moment is about to burst forth. Primal sorrow is the key, then and now. Albert Einstein said, "The release of the atom power has changed everything except our way of thinking … the solution to this problem lies in the heart of mankind." The abiding sorrow! The Lord's, Noah's, Ours.

There are nine countries with nuclear weapons, enough to obliterate life. Yet, no one has built a table that seats the heads of the nine countries. Such a table would be like Noah building an ark to save life on earth.

While the world teeters on the brink, can the nine countries with the weapons say from their hearts, "I'm sorry"? Can the nations which tested and deformed generations of children say, "I'm sorry"? Can the folks who made sure that the world now possesses millions of years of toxicity say, "I'm sorry"? Can the nation that has used these weapons in war say, "I'm sorry"? Sorrow, deep in the human heart, needs to be expressed now. Only a full-throated confession of what we have done can save us from ourselves.

Dear George,

Every time that you went to church, in the middle of the worship service was "the Confession of Sin." Usually that conjured up personal wrongs committed of one kind or another. Personal confessions. But wrongs done collectively, wrongs that stifled and harmed life for generations rarely have a place in Confession. Collective confession is an orphan.

In our culture, there is absolutely no place for confession in public. Politicians, businesspeople, military strategists, are loath to admit that they have caused harm. Their audiences, admirers and followers want nothing to do with regret. These people speak to the media, and through the media, and there is no advantage in displaying weakness by admitting to making a mistake. Thus, confession in almost every public sphere, except worship, is anathema. But confession is necessary to be truly human. As a matter of fact, the Good News in the Christian religion begins with the word "Repent!" If the strongest leaders, the ones with nuclear weapons, can't say two words, "I'm sorry," I fear that we will never make it through our atomic age.

WHAT DO YOU THINK? We never get far from the first question: "Should an atomic bomb be dropped by us?" We Americans estimated that the human nature of our enemy, which led to war, would also lead to surrender if we dropped the bomb. Afterwards we had to live with our own human nature dealing with our bombs. At this point, do we assume that we are "the good people" and deserve to possess the weapons for protection against "the bad people"? Do we assume that our human nature is different from the human nature of our enemies?

CHAPTER 9

"I Will Blot Out … "

Dear George,
There was a time toward the end of World War II when you fin-
ished fighting in Palau and were waiting for your Marine unit
to depart to fight in Japan. That would have been the bloodiest
of last-ditch battles, but you were ready to go. Then the atomic
bomb was dropped on Hiroshima, and the war was soon over,
and you returned home.

It always fascinated me that you could easily have died in
Japan had it not been for the bomb. Nevertheless, you spent the
rest of your life working for the abolition of nuclear weapons.

I once saw a dramatic video depicting a man in Hiroshima
using two pictures. In the first he was sitting on the pave-
ment just before the bomb blast in 1945. Then came the blast.
When the smoke cleared, the man was no longer. The only
thing left was a tiny spot of vapor. In the second picture he
had been "blotted out." That is the picture which comes to my
mind when I read in the Noah story that the Lord was determined to "blot out" all life on the face of the earth.

When I consider "the nightmare" of nuclear weapons, my
mind often returns to scenes and pictures of Japan. The following are personal remembrances of Japan and the musing
they inspire in me.

I have a friend from Hiroshima named Tomoko Watanabe. In 2015, she told me the story of her dear friend, Kiyoko Imori. When the atomic bomb hit Hiroshima in 1945, Kiyoko was an eleven-year-old girl in the sixth grade at Honkawa Elementary School which was about 400 yards from the epicenter of the destruction. Every child, teacher and staff member in the Honkawa Elementary School died instantly, everyone except Kiyoko Imori. She had temporarily stepped behind a wall when the bomb went off. In addition, her entire family was gone, as well. All beyond recognition.

In her teen years and as a young lady, what followed for her was a tumor in her pancreas, then thyroid cancer, then meningioma, and unremitting pain. Despite all of the diseases, Kiyoko married and was pregnant. Imagine the happy news! The possibility of Kiyoko giving birth and starting a family! But that was not to be. Miscarriage after miscarriage followed.

In 2015, seventy years after the bomb, Kioko lay in a hospital bed in Japan needing a dose of morphine every four hours, around the clock, to endure the pain inflicted on her in the Honkawa Elementary School, on August 6, 1945. In the hallways of her hospital, her voice could be heard crying out, "Please kill me."

I gave a speech about her at the United Nations on April 9, 2015. I said, "Who, today, makes the decisions about building more and more sophisticated nuclear weapons to target tomorrow's children? Of course, the experts do. The expert politicians and military strategists. But what do they know about nuclear-degraded life? What experience have they had in witnessing the effects of the weapons that they upgrade? Do they decide the way forward from an antiseptic, safe distance away from the reality of nuclear pain? Or do they listen to the nuclear lament such as the lament of Kiyoko as she mourns her unborn, and her vaporized classmates and annihilated family members and while she endures a lifetime of excruciating, unrelenting agony? I would wager that she learned more about nuclear weapons in the sixth grade at Honkawa Elementary School than all of today's experts in the nuclear nations. She knows what is important, and she carries that knowledge in her tiny body."

In 1966, I was part of an official delegation that went to Hiroshima and laid a peace wreath at a sacred memorial spot. Mary and I had some time to look around at the main gathering spot commemorating August 6, 1945. So, we went to a theater there to see a movie about the end of World War II. The beginning of the movie seemed to follow a recognizable script, but at the apex of the movie, the narrator made the most unsettling statement. I distinctly remember my reaction when the narrator said something like, "While Japan was engaged in a war in this region of the world, for some reason that we did not understand at the time and still don't understand, the United States of America dropped the atomic bomb on us."

Obviously, the narrator was correct that the United States dropped the first atomic bomb there, and it wreaked devastation on the people of Hiroshima. But the war that Japan had waged against so many people in so many counties and in such a brutal fashion was totally ignored. Context was completely ignored in favor of an assumption of innocence.

I remember immediately trying to read the book, *The Rape of Nanking* by Iris Chang. It recounted so many atrocities that the Japanese inflicted on the townspeople of Nanjing, China, that after one hundred pages, I became ill and had to abandon the book. Live human beings were tied to poles while the Japanese soldiers thrust their bayonets into their bodies for practice. It literally made me sick. Then to hear a breezy comment about being "engaged in a war in this region," and implying innocence startled me into thinking about Hiroshima in more complexity. The hearts of all involved are complicit.

One association with Hiroshima is close to home for me. Occasionally, these days, I will give someone a gold-leafed ginkgo leaf. A note goes with the gift that says:

Just before 1200 AD, Chinese monks introduced gingko trees to Japan. Some took root in Hiroshima.

In 1945, the atomic bomb wiped out all gingko trees in Hiroshima, all except four of these trees.

A few saplings from these surviving gingko trees were brought to San Francisco, California, in 2015. When these saplings were big enough, they were planted in the Japanese Tea Garden of Golden Gate Park on September 20, 2019, in honor of George and Charlotte Shultz.

On August 2, 2020, Mary and Bill Swing drove to the Japanese Tea Garden, and, with permission, picked one hundred gingko leaves to be gifts to commemorate the seventy-fifth anniversary of the atomic bombing of Hiroshima and Nagasaki.

These leaves were sent to Azusa, California, to have a craftsman supply them with gold leaf.

So, this golden gingko leaf has a long history. Now it is a gift of peace, endurance and hope to you.

Let us eliminate all of the warheads and live like gingko leaves, i.e., full of beauty and at one with the created order.

Finally, a most colorful and unforgettable memory of Japan comes to mind. While traveling the world to start the United Religions Initiative, through a series of "accidental" happenstances, I came to know and be involved with the Oomoto Shinto sect, one of Japan's "new religions." They are amazing people with a brave history and an inclusive theology. Over time, Mary and I visited their temple in Kameoka, near Kyoto. Over one winter break, we were invited to visit their winter retreat in the mountains at Ayabe.

On New Year's Eve, everyone in town was invited to write down, on little slips of paper, things that they had done wrong and place those slips of paper in large baskets. Priests from Oomoto, gathered the baskets, and hundreds of us processed through very deep snow following the priests to the Hozugawa River. Water from the roaring mountain stream thundered under the prominent, well-lit bridge while the priests emptied the baskets. We all watched the tiny white slips of paper descend into the night and the water and vanish. Breathtaking forgiveness!

The water certainly washed away the ink of the personal wrongs committed. But it would take a universal flood to wash away the hardheartedness concentrated in our nuclear arsenals.

Meanwhile, we are not absolved from the nightmare of nuclear weapons which landed first in Japan, nor from the nightmare of the holocaust that awaits to blot out the world's life. The regret that awaits is not local but cosmic.

Dear George,

Each year I go by the Japanese Tea Garden in San Francisco to see how the two gingko trees are doing and to harvest fresh leaves. I have given golden gingko leaves to people all over the world, and they all are deeply touched and most appreciative. You and Charlotte continue to inspire.

WHAT DO YOU THINK? Perhaps the story of the four gingko trees is similar to the Noah story, in that in the midst of seemingly complete devastation, a small remnant, nevertheless, survives, and over time, it flourishes. Is there a difference in your thinking between a world totally destroyed by nukes and a world in which a tiny cluster of life survives? Does it matter to you?

PART THREE

THE HOPE

Here is the scene: Our 13,000 nuclear warheads
have denotated, and the resulting cloud of smoke
totally engulfs your vision. Then the cloud begins
to break up and you begin to glimpse the first sight
of a post-atomic world. You say, "I hope … "

This is not a quick hope off the top of your head,
but a thoughtful hope that wells up from your
depths. Down where the inner force of your life
has driven you all these years. Down in this fertile,
soulful ground, now what is your hope?

CHAPTER 10

A New Heaven and a New Earth

Dear George,

Now we enter the blinding cloud of unknowing where we consider and embrace the end of all life, not just yours and mine. What happens to planet Earth at its conclusion? Will it end up being lifeless much longer than it was lively? Religious imagination/revelation/prophecies suggest that whatever the answer, it will not come without tribulation. Yet, tribulation isn't the final word. Hope is.

Today we have "the fog of atomic darkness that hovers so pervasively over our Earth, God's Earth," as we say in the Voices Nuclear Prayer. We anticipate the coming mushroom clouds that will surely come in time and likely extinguish life, wholesale, on this planet. We rightfully flinch at the awaiting horror. But maybe on the other side of the coming tribulation is the birth of a new heaven and a new Earth.

Mikhail Gorbachev and Ronald Reagan issued a statement saying that "a nuclear war cannot be won and therefore must never be fought." That was in 1985. Now, in 2023, I consider that the nuclear war has already begun. In 2023!

Today, military strategists play "war games" in deadly earnest, ready to make them operational. Taxpayers underwrite billions of dollars in the fight for this nuclear war effort. Heads of states bluff and threaten each other with nuclear weapons while the world holds its breath. Nuclear wartime propaganda proliferates in political campaigns and "saber-rattling" speeches. Nuclear-armed nations jealously hold onto the right to bomb first. All of this and much more are required in our present-day nuclear war which has taken seventy-eight years to prepare for and will take only a very short battle to execute. Our ultimately consequential very short time! We were not around for "the big bang at the beginning," but we are doing what we can to hasten "the big bang at the end." The fuse is in place waiting for a match.

Throughout history, various people have proclaimed that the end of the world was at hand. And they were wrong. Their assumption usually was that God would bring the end. Today, humankind has the power to bring the end. This moment, the summer of 2023, and this context are different from the years before the nuclear war that I see unfolding now.

Oppenheimer, a man of advanced science, understood what he was doing with atom bombs. He put it in religious terms saying, "So death doth touch resurrection." The atomic age has only one ending point, namely annihilation. Therefore, the only hope is resurrection. As a "man of the cloth," I look at our perilous moment today and try to find a myth, an allegory, a metaphor, an ancient tale, or a vision that speaks to my soulful dread. Looking for any kind of hope, like Oppenheimer, I turn to the Book of Revelation.

Please understand, the Book of Revelation is severely complicated. One of my seminary professors in the late 1950s said, "No one under the age of forty should be allowed to read the Book of Revelation." I get his point when talking about the entire book. But amidst all of the needed exegesis are a few breathtaking visions. The one that comes to me right now is this:

"Then I saw a new heaven and a new earth; for the first heaven and the first earth had passed away ... And I saw the holy city, the new Jerusalem, coming down out of heaven from God ... And the one who was seated on the throne said, "Behold, I am making all things new." (Book of Revelation 21:1-5)

Yes, it would be easy in the summer of 2023 to dismiss these words because of the imagery of "one on the throne." Or because of the use of the word "he." Or because Jerusalem is the focus, thus rendering Hindus and Muslims and all the others out of the picture. But what resonates with me is not the literal imagery. What engages my heart is the poetic picture of a cosmic regime change. What if everything ended, and what if an entirely new dimension of reality came into being? Not hope on a small, "get me through the night" scale, but hope on an apocalyptic scale. Can we hope that life is not negated by a bomb, but rather that the universe's Originating Force ushers in an expanded dimension of life after the bomb?

Wouldn't it be the supreme irony if the nuclear bombs which betrayed all life on this planet ended up being the agents for fuller life beyond our present realm? Nuclear weapons would then be seen as the necessary villain in the passion play of our destiny, much like Judas Iscariot—who some of us consider to be the pioneer of a "cosmic regime change" and prototype of the next iteration of life—was the necessary villain in the passion story of Jesus. If so, then the first bomb, called "Little Boy," could well have been called Judas Iscariot.

WHAT DO YOU THINK? Before the bombs were dropped, human beings had never faced the prospect of an atomic cloud over their heads. Now we live with it as well as with a cloud of atomic darkness in our hearts. Nevertheless, we are people of inveterate hope. What are your highest hopes for our atomic age? Continuity or discontinuity? The age of the human?

CHAPTER 11

For the First Heaven … Passed Away

What did "the first heaven" look like? The one that is going to pass away.

No one has ever taken pictures of "the first heaven." Heaven is not a place. Instead, it is a conjured state, an invisible realm which is the product of folk tales, fond yearnings and declarations of revelations. Such vagueness does not mean that there is no truth to the notions about heaven. It simply means that heaven is not an exterior place which can be measured, but rather an interior hope that can grip our imagination. Hope!

Not long ago, I was talking with someone whose spouse had died suddenly and unexpectedly. I asked, "where do you think that your husband is right now?" Without hesitation she said that he was reunited with his family members who had gone before. The clear and unvarnished response was so forthcoming that I figured that it was shared by tribal people, ancestor worship people the world over, and people throughout time. Shared in hearts, not books.

Hope addresses the hard question of "what next?" And the answer often is "heaven." Heaven is commonly assumed by the world's religions to be the place of final accountability. Our only hope in our "closing argument" before the throne of God will be a plea for mercy.

If we folks living today struggle so heroically with the issues of right and wrong, shouldn't there be a final reckoning somewhere? In heaven? A final reckoning place is part of the heaven that many people of this world hope for.

Did you know that in heaven there was a war? Not really, but it is in the Book of Revelation, which says, "And war broke out in heaven; Michael and his angels fought against the dragon. The dragon and his angels fought back, but they were defeated, and there was no longer any place for them in heaven. The great dragon was thrown down, that ancient serpent, who is called the devil and Satan, the deceiver of the whole world—he was thrown down to the earth, and his angels were thrown down with him … woe to the earth and the sea for the devil has come down to you with great wrath, because he knows that his time is short." (Revelation 12:7-12)

Keep in mind that this story is from the Book of Revelation. Without taking it too literally, I find two themes to be interesting. First, heaven has not always been a static place. A war and fighting took place there, for heaven's sake. Second, although there once was room for Satan in heaven, after the war, there was "no longer any place for him in heaven." Thus, heaven seems to be the place where the tension and fever between God and Satan was broken. A place now "where God will be all in all."

Here are some questions and comments that rattle around in my brain as I think about the first heaven which is fading into irrelevance. Just random personal musings. Here are my own "frequently asked questions (FAQs)" and immediate comments.

1. What if there is no heaven? Comment: Never-

theless, we will make one up to give us hope.

2. When did heaven start? Comment: Perhaps 4.5 billion years ago with Earth's creation in the big bang, a vision of heaven was implanted in our inner beings. Or did heaven start 150,000 years ago with the advent of mammals and perhaps otherworldly aspirations?

3. Do dogs go to heaven? Comment: I hope the ones that bite don't make it.

4. If only humans go to heaven, what if there is "life" on other planets? Comment: Would we all go to the same heaven, or will there be separate heavens for people of different planets?

5. If, as the Book of Revelation says, "the first heaven will pass away," what happens to the people in that first heaven? Comment: Do they get preferential treatment in the new heaven, or do they lose out altogether?

6. Is hell the opposite of heaven, the undesirable neighborhood of the afterlife where "bad" people are forced to live forever? Comment: Eternity without mercy would make one question the heart of the creator/judge. It has to be "heaven or bust." Hell could not have a future.

7. Do only *Homo sapiens* go to heaven? Comment:

What about the *Australopithecus*, the *Homo habilis*, the *Homo erectus*, the *Homo neanderthalensis*? Do they make the cut or is heaven only for the likes of us, *Homo sapiens* (Translation: the wise humans)? Comment: Oh, my goodness, that raises the question of evolution, namely, are there more degrees of evolution ahead—beyond *Homo sapiens*—ready to emerge on earth? Thus, requiring us to wait in line with the *Homo neanderthalensis* for heaven and hope for the best. (A study published by the University of Bristol in September 2023 claims that mammals have been around about 150,000 years and will likely only make it for about 150,000 more years. Time might be running out for *Homo sapiens* to qualify for heaven regardless of a nuclear holocaust.)

8. Will there be nuclear weapons in heaven? Comment: then it wouldn't be heaven; it would be New Mexico.

9. Do people who do not believe that there is a heaven get to go to heaven, anyway? Comment: Like the answer to every question above and all the obvious questions that might follow, heaven exists only in the mind of God, not in our wishful imaginings. If there is a heaven, it would be God's domain to determine its clientele.

Maybe all of us have "got it wrong" when we speak about heaven? Maybe our first heaven just passes away?

As for clues about heaven from the words of Jesus, I only want to mention two. First, heaven appears at the beginning of the Lord's Prayer: "Our Father who art in heaven." (Matthew 6:9) In theological terms, heaven is God's domain. We can imagine all we want, but we don't know. Heaven belongs to God and not to us.

Second, Jesus said, "For in the resurrection they neither marry nor are given in marriage but are like angels in heaven." (Matthew 22:30) So, in heaven there is no more sex or jealousy or intimacy or fighting or enduring bonding or anything that we can conjure up. Heaven is a place for the totally, unthinkably different.

Whimsically, I think that when we get to "the pearly gates," we all receive report cards on how we did on earth. Anxiously we open the report cards only to discover that we all received the same grade, "Incomplete." Divine mercy alone can bring any of us up to a passing grade.

A serious and totally different consideration of heaven can be found in Leo Tolstoy's book, *The Kingdom of Heaven is Within You.* Not out in the cosmos but inward, inside one's heart and soul. In this 1894 book, he wrote of his disgust with his so-called Christian nation of Russia with its "prisons ... constantly increasing armaments and millions of confused people ready, like trained hounds, to attack anyone against whom their masters set them. This situation ... is above all the product of public opinion."

The antidote that Tolstoy espoused was for people to turn inside themselves and discover the Kingdom of Heaven that abides there. "The Kingdom of Heaven Is Within You." Love truth, honor God, trust all people as your family. Tolstoy became a Christian and was convinced that orthodox Christianity in his day was corrupt and anti-Christian. Therefore, he called for Christians to reject doctrines, church institutions, and hierarchies. Regarding governments, he called for nonresistance to evil—an idea that made a profound impression on Gandhi, and in turn, became a vital part of Indian independence. Martin Luther King, Jr. picked up this theme of nonresistance or passive resistance and had a profound effect on the United States. Nonresistance also had an effect on Dorothy Day and the Catholic Worker Movement in the United States.

Billions of people throughout history have been influenced by the concept of heaven, the first heaven which, according to the Book of Revelation, will pass away, whether that heaven is beyond the stratosphere or in the human heart or in the mind of God.

Dear George,

Every morning before breakfast I say a little prayer and end with "In the high vault of heaven, glory to You." I realize that it doesn't make any rational sense that there is a place called heaven and that it has high ceilings. Nevertheless, this brief devotional thought captures something far beyond my breakfast table, something that attracts my heart. I sense that in this vast universe there is a Divine Presence worthy of praise, even from me, as tiny and remote as I am. So, my imperfect prayer hints of a realm of staggering grandeur far beyond my comprehension, "in the high vault of heaven."

WHAT DO YOU THINK? The cooking show hostess, Julia Child used to say, "This dessert is heavenly." The dancer, actor, and singer Fred Astaire used to sing, "Heaven. I'm in heaven and

I seem to find the happiness I seek, when we're out together dancing cheek to cheek." Does your vision of heaven go deeper than a dessert or a dance song? Do you take heaven seriously? How so? Does it have any relevance to the way you live?

CHAPTER 12

For the First Earth … Passed Away

Dear George,

I carry with me several poignant scenes surrounding your death and Charlotte's death, when you "passed away."

On Saturday, May 1, 2021, at your interment, our contingent left the Shultz farmhouse in Western Massachusetts. Charlotte, your children, and grandchildren, and families. The local police, the state police, and Marines. We followed the hearse down the hill and into the little village of Cummington. We looked out the car windows and saw every person in town—from tiny children to tottering elderly—lining the road and silently holding American flags, in tribute to you! I still weep when I remember.

Then we all went up Potash Hill Road to the Dawes Cemetery. A cold wind blew through the temporary tent, and a very thin and ill Charlotte shivered. I said, "I welcome the family and friends of George Pratt Shultz to this service of interment. The years of his life spanned a century and the reach of his influence stretched to all parts of the world. Now, at the end, his body will rest at peace among his beloved ancestors and dear kin." There was a Marine flyover and a final blessing.

Not long afterwards, Charlotte died. Twenty-four members of her family gathered at Pier 26 in San Francisco on Friday afternoon, January 14, 2022. Ranking members of the fire department greeted us and escorted us onto Fire Boat 3. Members of the Fire Boat 3 crew helped each one of us grab a rope and swing onto the boat. Then off we went toward the Golden Gate Bridge.

Our worst fear had been that this January day would be windy and rainy. Previously Charlotte had requested that her ashes be scattered beneath the Golden Gate Bridge at sunset. So, we picked a date and hoped for the best.

Thankfully, it was a calm and sunny evening. After sailing out toward the headlands, Fire Boat 3 settled under the Golden Gate Bridge, and the box containing her ashes was opened. I said:

> So, we stand here, at the last, with Charlotte's ashes and with abiding affection for her.
>
> Imagine her as a radiant youth in Borger, Texas.
>
> Remember how she poured her soul into the life of this great city.
>
> Admire how she recovered from illnesses and accidents with ferocious will power.
>
> Be grateful that she loved us.
>
> It is our distinct honor to be here at the end of Charlotte's earthly pilgrimage and to give her a fond farewell as she begins her unfathomable journey into the arms of God.

A brief liturgy followed. At the words, "Even at the grave we make our song, Alleluia, Alleluia, Alleluia," I added, "and Charlotte makes her song, 'I Left My Heart in San Francisco.'"

When the last of her ashes blended into San Francisco Bay, the impressive horn of Fireboat 3 gave out three long salutes, *the horizon turned red and golden, the spray from the water canon guided us toward Pier 26, the moon glistened off the alabaster buildings of San Francisco. And we all watched in awe. Charlotte!*

Life on planet Earth will come to an end. Not just ours but the entire planet's life.

The theme of the world coming to an end is biblical, found throughout the scriptures, and is clearly a Christian theme. Classic Christian theology has five categories: Creation, The Fall, Redemption, The Spirit/Church, and The End. Yes, the end of this world as we know it. Such theology takes for granted that all life on this planet is temporary.

LONG VIEW

Although astronomers have often spoken about the possibility of a star eating a planet, it was pure conjecture until now. Kishalay De, a post-doctoral fellow at MIT's Kavli Institute for Astrophysics and Space Research, observed a star that was beginning to run out of fuel and beginning to bloat. As it swelled in size, the star's outer atmosphere came into contact with an orbiting planet which was filled with gas. As the planet, in its orbit, got closer to the star, the planet plunged into the star which immediately ballooned up before returning to its previous size.

Stars eat planets the size of Mercury or Jupiter and could eat Earth, according to an article in the May 3, 2023, issue of the journal, *Nature*. Mansi Kasliwal, a professor of astronomy at Caltech says, "Truth be told, we won't be around to see this happen. We won't be on planet Earth to see this." Because long before Earth gets swallowed, the increasing heat output from our sun will have evaporated all of Earth's water and rendered the planet uninhabitable. "We will have to find a new home long before this happens," she says. Astrophysicist Smadar Naoz is quoted in the same article observing, "Whether or not the sun will engulf the Earth is quite controversial. But it won't matter because it will no longer be our beautiful Earth with an atmosphere and oceans."

NOT SO LONG VIEW

Geoffrey Hinton, an Emeritus Professor at the University of Toronto, an engineering fellow at Google, and the so-called "godfather of AI," gave a sobering lecture reported by CBS on May 25, 2023. In it he said that he now believes that he underestimated the existential threat that artificial intelligence (AI) and chatbots pose. "Once AI can create its own goals, humans won't be needed. Humanity is just a passing phase of evolutionary intelligence." In other words, we don't have much more time.

Author and former Google executive Mo Gawdat was quoted in the May 19, 2023, *New York Post* saying that artificial intelligence machines could one day view humans as "scum" and could create killing machines to rid the world of them. Gawdat did say, "That day is still a bit away."

Listening to Gawdat and Hinton, I think I can hear echoes of Oppenheimer and Sakharov saying in horror that we have created something that can annihilate life on a massive scale.

Chemical and biological threats could get out of hand and take us to a stage of destruction that would make a pandemic pale by comparison. As for the effects of global warming, the first harvest of our pollution lives in our disturbing weather patterns.

TODAY/NOW

Nine countries, with a handful of enemies, have made friends with 13,000 nuclear warheads. But 13,000 weapons have only one enemy, namely planet Earth. People use these weapons to bluff one another, but the cosmic result of using them is that life on this earth will pass away.

Mass extinction is nothing new to planet Earth. In a 2020 article on the ThoughtCo reference website, writer Heather Scoville asserts that in the 4.6 billion years of life forms on earth, there have been "five major mass extinction events that wiped out an overwhelming majority of species living at that time." During the Ordovician Mass Extinction, about 440 million years ago, about 85 percent of species were eliminated. During the Devonian Mass Extinction, about 375 million years ago, about 80 percent of species were eliminated. During the Permian Mass Extinction, about 250 million years ago, nearly 96 percent of species were eliminated. During the Triassic-Jurassic Mass Extinction, about 200 million years ago, more than 50 percent of species were eliminated. And during the K-T Mass Extinction, about 65 million years ago, about 75 percent of species were eliminated. What if in our atomic age, the age of the human, we built weapons strong enough for mass extinction? Based on our technologically advanced thinking and our spiritual depravity?

Since the mythical Adam and Eve left the Garden of Eden, human beings have not only struggled to navigate a world of injustice, pain and death, but also have found ways of tapping into beauty, human compassion, music, and wondrous creativity. Until now, the promising earth seemed like a fitting and endless arena for our deepest hopes. Until now! Our "now" can be summed up in the lyrics of the John Denver song, "Let Us Begin (What Are We Making Weapons For?)" that say, "For the first time, this might be the last time."

Here we are peering into a future that might have no place for the likes of us or our descendants. Perhaps feeling that we are riding on an orb that has an expiration date, what do we do? Drugs? Dreams? Delusions? Or Poems? Prayers? Promises? We try to latch onto the universe, our hope of last resort.

I found the big winner of the 2023 Academy Awards, *Everything Everywhere All At Once*, to offer a fascinating commentary on this moment. The heroine finds everything in her life is falling apart, so, she dreams, and she begins to understand that her existence—and all existence?—is descending into chaos. Her hope is to enter multiple parallel universes and allow her many selves to absorb various skills in a variety of dimensions. A cinematic hope that unless the universe(s) can come to our aid, the heaviness of life will do us in!

When an individual comes smack up against the truth that he or she will die and be gone, then the individual begins to imagine a "post-me world." That is the time to make a will, express last wishes and describe where last remains are to be located. Magnify that scenario by trillions and the time comes when we need to consider a "post-world world." If life goes out of this planet, then where will life be located in the universe? Will I or my descendants have any relationship with the arc of life unfolding amid the birthing stars and planets?

WHAT DO YOU THINK? Tombstones are usually etched with a few words, a thought that seeks to memorialize a unique quality of the deceased. If you wrote an epitaph on the gravestone of our planet, what words would you write?

CHAPTER 13

Meanwhile, Our Best Hopes

Dear George,
I have spoken about nuclear weapons on the East Coast, the
Midwest and the West Coast, and always the first question
posed to me is, "Where is the hope?" It is an understandable
question. So much so that most people I encounter can't imagine
an answer, and so they don't want to think about the subject.

In the final scene of the Oppenheimer *movie, Oppen-*
heimer says to Einstein, "Albert, when I came to you with these
calculations, we were worried that we'd start a chain reaction
that would destroy the entire world." Einstein replies, "I remem-
ber it well. What of it?" Oppenheimer says, "I believe we did."

Then the screenplay calls for a close-up of Oppenheimer
with the camera on his eyes as he visualizes the expanding
nuclear arsenals of the world. When he can take it no longer,
the script calls for the actor to "JAM his eyes closed."

If it was true that J. Robert Oppenheimer jammed his eyes
closed when he imagined what was coming, it has to be a reflex
for us who glimpse now what he glimpsed then. We, too, want
to jam our eyes closed because our situation of living with these
weapons seems hopeless.

What hope did J. Robert Oppenheimer have when the bombs
were deployed on Hiroshima and Nagasaki? In his farewell

"Speech to the Association of Los Alamos Scientists" on November 2, 1945, he spoke of his hope for a new world order.

"The point is that atomic weapons constitute also a field, a new field, and a new opportunity for realizing preconditions," he said. "Atomic weapons are a peril which affect everyone in the world, and in that sense [are] a completely common problem ... I think that to handle this common problem there must be a complete sense of community responsibility ... The only unique end can be a world that is united, and a world in which war will not occur ... The one point I want to hammer home is what an enormous change in spirit is involved ... And when I speak of a new spirit in international affairs, I mean that ... there is something more profound than [even the deepest things that Americans cherish and would die for]; namely, the common bond with other men everywhere."

Today, the hope that Oppenheimer envisaged—a world without war, a world in which a common bond develops between all people, and a world linked through a new spirit— seems staggeringly naïve. But what is he saying? He is saying that such weapons must create a new world, or else! The weapons are not going away. Even greater weapons will follow in their wake. This new world of new weapons requires everyone to come together to save all life. Like a planet-destroying monster has now been created, and the only way to restrain the monster is for everyone on Earth, out of self-preservation or planet preservation, to hold the monster in check. How to do that? By destroying the monster? Or by developing safeguards to enchain the monster?

Oppenheimer's hope is not far from my hope. And the hopes of hundreds, perhaps thousands of groups worldwide who advocate daily for the abolition of nuclear weapons. We know that a global consensus against these weapons must be forged in order to save this planet. Scientists, physicians, artists, humanitarians, and scores of others around the world are trying to create a global plurality that will override the nine political units that control the monster and use it to threaten others for political or national or personal gain.

Amid this deadly serious global drama, where is the hope? I can imagine five categories of hopes and their expression:

PERSONAL

"I hope that I die before the big bombs go off."

"In the coming nuclear war, I hope that the good guys win, and the bad guys lose."

"I hope that the way things are now, which seems to be working, keeps on working forever."

"When the bombs go off, I hope that I am at ground zero and not on the periphery where the suffering will be agonizing."

"I hope that the whole matter will just go away."

"I hope that a limited (tactical) nuclear bomb goes off and wakes up the world as to what is really going on with these weapons."

INTERNATIONAL

"I hope that the nine nuclear-armed nations will talk with each other about the weapons and agree on a path of safety for life on this earth."

"I hope that the nuclear weapons abolition groups of the world can come together and discover a single voice and become a compelling force."

"I hope that number of warheads (about 13,000) can be reduced to 1,000."

"I hope that the nine nuclear-armed nations follow the example of South Africa, which is the world's only country to achieve nuclear weapons capability, and then voluntarily relinquish it."

"I hope that a sense of planet security will be recognized as more important than any nation's security."

"I hope that the nuclear-armed nations would abide by and not try to skirt the Non-Proliferation Treaty which calls for "complete disarmament under strict and effective control."

EVOLUTIONAL

"I hope that long after the nuclear bombs go off, there will be enough human beings left on earth to keep our species alive."

"I hope that robots 'will not replace us' in the post-bomb age."

"I hope that Earth will not be a lifeless planet."

"I hope that human life on Earth will live long enough to help our species evolve into fuller being."

"I hope that all of us creatures can adhere to a 'Declaration of Mutual Interdependence,' instead of having to live by a pact of 'Mutually Assured Destruction.'"

COSMIC

"I hope that some of us can fly away to another planet before the bombing starts."

"I hope that there is human-like life on other planets, so even if we disappear, they will carry on."

"I hope that creatures in a spaceship will come and save us." (Edgar Mitchell, the sixth person to walk on the moon, was convinced that extraterrestrials were already here neutralizing our bombs.)

Science fiction engages young minds in cosmic possibilities. For instance, futuristic author, Octavia E. Butler, in her novel *Parable of the Sower*, presents a heroine who is asleep aboard a vast spaceship, haunted by confusing memories of a nuclear war that ravaged her planet. Now she is being held captive by a benevolent alien race that intervened in the human race's extinction. After rescuing the survivors and placing them in a coma-like sleep for centuries, they awake and are ready to rebuild a restored Earth.

RESURRECTION

This hope will be addressed in the following chapters.

WHAT DO YOU THINK? We have lived with nuclear weapons for seventy-eight years. At some deep level, we are aware of them and their potential. Yet we tolerate (perhaps celebrate) them and explicitly—through paying taxes—support their existence and expansion. We could not live with such dangers unless we hoped that something good would come from them. What is that good for you, and what is your deepest hope given that these weapons are currently in our possession?

CHAPTER 14

A Far-Out Hope—Cosmic Humility

Dear George,

In 2016, when Good Friday was approaching, you asked me a direct question: what was Jesus like approaching his death? This is what I wrote to you in reply:

> *I mentioned that his attention focused on what was immediately ahead and what was at stake. No miracles! He stopped teaching. People stopped asking him questions. He almost stopped talking to the apostles. He was single minded, and he prayed to his Father more than talked with disciples. The content of his prayers (how in the world was that ever recorded?) became central to the story. Clearly his conversations turned from human dialogue to Divine dialogue.*
>
> *What was immediately ahead? The painful prospect of being crucified.*
>
> *What was at stake? Ah, there is the question. In those days, he spoke in agrarian terms. Seeds! 'As for what you sow, you do not sow the body that is to be, but you sow a bare seed ... But God gives it a body ...' Elsewhere it is written, 'So it is in the resurrection. What is sown is perishable, what is raised is imperishable.' Still elsewhere, 'I tell you a mystery. We will all be changed.'*

He is about to forge into a dimension that has cosmic consequences. This was not about a moment of religious history or the immortality of his soul. This was about ushering in an entirely new dimension of life. This was about pioneering a realm which could not be seen with a telescope. He was the seed that God would sow in a domain that presently was invisible and unimaginable.

Were he living in today's world, I'll bet he would have harkened back to the big bang when the entire universe was created in less than a blink—and it all came from a singularity of less than a tablespoon in size. From one singularity or seed, through the miracles of expansion and gravity, the 'old' universe came together and held together. As he approached his death, he sweated his coming passion believing that on the other side was the New Creation ... or the Kingdom of God.

I hope that you and Charlotte have a deep Good Friday and a joyful Easter, Bill.

Perhaps we are seeing ourselves through a tiny, myopic lens. What if we saw ourselves in a far greater context? Would that better inform our hope? Positively or negatively?

In the summer of 2022, when we looked up into the sky, something new was up there, the James Webb Space Telescope. It was performing a halo orbit, circling around a point in space known as the "Sun-Earth L2 Lagrange Point," about a million miles away.

From there, astronomers have been searching for light

from the first stars, from the first galaxies formed in the big bang over 13 billion years ago. They have been searching for the origins of life.

Scientists were also using this spot to get as close as possible to instances of planetary deaths. It is hard to take this in. They are looking for answers to the questions: how did Earth start? How will Earth end?

What they saw was a cosmic maternity ward where stars are being born. Also, they saw a cosmic graveyard where dead planets drift along in arid quiet. Both timed in terms of millions of light years! Earth fits somewhere in between the maternity ward and the graveyard but definitely trending toward the graveyard.

Not too many centuries ago, we assumed that Earth was the center of the universe, and everything revolved around Earth and us. "Man is the measure of all things," proclaimed the ancient Greek philosopher Protagoras of Abdera, a contemporary of Sophocles. Now we are trying to adapt to the reality that our basic understanding of the big picture was totally wrong.

Now we realize that we are only a small planet in a vast complex of constantly expanding galaxies. There are 4 trillion galaxies in the visible universe … 11 billion Earth-like planets in the Milky Way. We are so infinitely tiny that we might adopt the one needed characteristic: cosmic humility. Without it, we will continue to arm our inflated, erroneous estimates of our place in the universe.

We aren't the masters of our fate. We are tenders of our little garden. We aren't an endless line of warring tribal chieftains. We are kindergarteners in a sandbox trying to learn to share. Or else!

Our planet is not a bottomless boon for exploitation. Earth is our first, last, and only chance of sustaining human life on a little planet. Just enough oxygen, just the right temperature! But we need just enough perspective.

Mikhail Gorbachev once said, "I believe in the cosmos. All of us are linked to the cosmos." If we are enslaved creatures chained to the overriding needs of national security, then nuclear weapons create our ultimate destiny. "He who lives by the sword, dies by the sword." But if we could glimpse our place in the universe, we could make ultimate decisions based on the survival of the entire planet Earth. Cosmic humility can bring us hope.

WHAT DO YOU THINK? Millions upon millions of people are ready to die for the sovereignty of their country and to kill others for the sake of their nation's security. This is patriotism at its most brutal and essential level. But when you add nuclear weapons as a means of expressing patriotism, we are at another level entirely. If your patriotism, augmented with nuclear weapons, calls for the use of these weapons, are you willing to destroy life on earth to protect your nation's sovereignty? Or do you "draw a line in the sand"? Where is that line for you?

CHAPTER 15

The Final Hope—A New Jerusalem

The Book of Revelation culminates in a peaceful vision of Jerusalem, of all unlikely places. Yes, the word for peace (salem or shalom or salaam) is part of the word Jerusalem. And yes, there are any number of biblical passages associating Jerusalem with peace. But in truth, Jerusalem has been fought over sixteen times; destroyed two times; besieged twenty-three times; attacked fifty-two times; and captured and recaptured forty-four times. One must have an expansive concept of peace to make the peace leap to Jerusalem.

When visiting Jerusalem, the modern-day tourist or pilgrim might go to the wall around the Old City and enter the Tower of David Museum. This utterly fascinating place keeps the history—architecturally—of the last 3,000 years of the city's trials, bloodshed, and victories. Victories by ancient Canaanites, Judeans, Jebusites, Egyptians, Assyrians, Babylonians, Persians, Macedonians, Romans, Syrians, and Greeks. More recently Ottoman Turks and others have flown their flags or made their claims over this city.

Even today, with the Hamas/Israeli bloodbath, Jerusalem is often in the news because of sectarian violence and heightened tensions, not because it is a paragon of peace. Three major religions of the world have anchors and tragic histories in Jerusalem. So, one of the meanings of "the new Jerusalem coming down out of heaven," is that if peace can "make it there, it can make it anywhere," as the song goes.

The author of the Book of Revelation was aware of empires and kingdoms and extremely aware of the religious significance of Jerusalem. From his island home of Patmos, he wrote, "I was in the spirit on the Lord's day, and I heard behind me a loud voice saying, 'Write!'" (Book of Revelation 1:9,10) The culmination of all that he wrote was the vision of the new Jerusalem, a city at peace with itself. (Book of Revelation 21:2-4)

Why should anyone at this moment give any notice, or credence, to someone writing "in the spirit" two thousand years ago? At least, it might be interesting. At most, with the bombs of finality poised to go off, we need to research all revered insights about the final scene of life on this earth. It is not the time to simply "change the channel" or pick the best dog in the show. This moment demands total vision: telescope watchers, mystic visionaries, astrophysicists, ethicists, sci-fi creators, and artists. It is far too late to hide from end-time insights regardless of their origins. What is the big picture?

What comes after The End?

I'll stay with the author of the Book of Revelation because the picture he paints hangs in the gallery of my deepest convictions, especially regarding nuclear weapons.

I think that the "business as usual" approach to nuclear weapons is going to get us all killed. We love to have the biggest weapons. To strut. To threaten. To be feared. To have prestige. To control the levers of power. To hide behind "national security interests" and make lots of money even if we must pollute the earth for millions of years. To declare that "if we don't, they will." To utter heroic words and then do all in our power to keep from enforcing them. But this is who we are, and who we are is about to destroy what there is of us on earth. We don't suffer from a bad attitude. This little planet will go dark because we are who we are. Who we are is the nuclear issue! We must own our inherent, voracious depravity. Owning up must come first. Can this world's nuclear annihilators repent—say we are wrong and move in the opposite direction? What are the chances?

There must be an intervention of supernatural proportions if "the meek will inherit the earth." (Matthew 5:5) After our bombs go off, we will not be "pulling ourselves up by our bootstraps." Our next of kin will be roaches. Evolution will be a joke, at the last, as will the concept of "the survival of the fittest." We are a danger to ourselves when we tolerate these weapons.

"Giving nuclear weapons to fiercely competing nations is like throwing razor blades into a playpen full of children," says my friend Jonathan Granoff, a lawyer, author, international advocate, and President of the Global Security Institute.

In my opinion, owning up to who we are and looking for an intervention of supernatural proportions represent our final and best hope both for Jerusalem of the Middle East and for the New Jerusalem "coming down out of heaven." Our nuclear weapons today do not represent a revised Cuban Missile Crisis. Our weapons are more powerful than those of 1962 and their devastation is immensely more consequential. We have entered an apocalyptic crisis where the Beginning and the End fuse into one and can be glimpsed through a telescope, or an awakened reality check of the human soul.

Dear George,

You and Reagan and Gorbachev and Oppenheimer and Sakharov looked into the future and saw the same thing: In time, the possibility of death in apocalyptic dimensions. The time will eventually come when the weapons created will outdistance human beings' ability to restrain them. It is one thing to ignite the first nuclear bomb, named "Little Boy," to stop a war; in time, this "Little Boy" will become, as the French say, "enfant terrible." It will be another thing entirely when these weapons proliferate and grow up to be able to cancel all life on earth, thus bringing an end to the war against creation by destroying it!

Such dire potential drives theologians to muse in the field of eschatology, the science of last things. It is concerned with death, with judgment, and with the final destiny of the soul, humankind, and creatures.

Finally, is life no more than the birth and death of planets and stars, with the likes of us merely along for the ride? A short ride, at that? Is there more to life than can be seen through a telescope? Do we matter? Is there a force in the universe, a force that cares? Are we just the tip of a firecracker that goes off in a little blaze into nothingness? Are we merely seeds of mistaken immortality blown into the cracks and crevices of Earth's hard surfaces, blooming for a moment but destined only for dust?

WHAT DO YOU THINK? Do you think that there will ever be peace in Jerusalem? Will the three religions located there come together to offer an example of peace? Today, amid the fighting in the Jerusalem area, the world has not witnessed one incident of peacemaking there by the Jewish, Christian and Muslim leaders together. What if nuclear weapons eventually get into the hands of all three religious groups? Can they be trusted to be faithful stewards when nuclear weapons are available? In the end, are nuclear weapons the ultimate test of religions? Is Jerusalem "a canary in the coal mine?"

CHAPTER 16

Heaven and Earth, Together at Last

Dear George,
We now enter the rapids, the swift current of total annihilation
and complete resurrection. This scene is, in my opinion, played
out in the final days of Jesus in Jerusalem. I look at this scene in
two distinct ways.

As a Christian, I see Jesus on a cross, and he is carrying
with him the full weight of the personal misdeeds of all indi-
viduals, the collective wrongs of all societies, and the heinous
crimes that have dotted all lands in all times. With his death,
all the above misdeeds die, and with his resurrection appear-
ances, the finality of the unfathomably unblemished day of fresh
existence arrives. He represents the pivot from the old way of
being, and he pioneers the new and enduring dimension of life.
For me, Jesus isn't just a religious person in history, although he
is undeniably that. He is, for me, the necessary, permanent and
promiscuously loving guide from the realm of all the old deaths
to the realm of all the new lives.

As an interfaith leader, I realize that billions of people of
other religions see Jesus differently than I do. I am not out to
convert them. I am out to make common cause with them in
serving this world together wherever we can. For me it is enough
that we share a respect for sacred differences. As for a cosmic
shift from this life to another, everyone is entitled to his or her

vision of ultimate reality. Thomas Jefferson once wrote, "It does me no injury for my neighbor to say there are twenty gods or no god. It neither picks my pocket nor breaks my leg."

With the possibility of life on earth ending, I intend to be alert to the eschatology of other religions. Perhaps there is some overlap or common ground in addressing the question "what's next?" Undoubtedly, I have much to learn on this score from the other faiths.

Scientists, politicians, and military leaders take us down the road to the end, but no farther. After the end, they (and we) draw a blank and are speechless. Nine nations spend endless amounts of money, invest in countless wacky and wicked strategies, have the weapons on trigger ready, possess the power to end all life; and then when all life is ended, they have led us to nothing. What next? They have no next in their thinking or capacity. Next is beyond their transient goals. All they want is our vote, money, and admiration. All we get is deadly pollution for a million years.

In the West, thinking about the damage done by Covid-19, we can work up a significant rage postulating that the Covid-19 virus emanated from a lab in Wuhan, China. But we don't have moral anger toward our own creation of nuclear weapons in New Mexico. Over ninety-eight percent of those infected with the coronavirus will recover. Zero percent of the people targeted by a nuclear bomb will survive.

Consider Stanley Kubrick's award-winning movie, *Dr. Strangelove: Or How I learned To Stop Worrying and Love the Bomb.* This hilarious satire from 1964 builds on the Cold War fixation that the public had with the prospects of a nuclear confrontation between the United States and the

Soviet Union. After a series of wild misadventures, Major T. J. "King" Kong enters the bomb bay, and sits on a hydrogen bomb as he tries to repair the electrical wiring. When the bomb bay opens, he jubilantly rides the hydrogen bomb as it descends on Russia.

The implication is that the feared nuclear war was about to begin by way of our gleeful bungling. What stupidity! Life would seemingly end on this planet. In the movie, there was silly talk about underground areas to hide in, but it was all a lark. The "what next?" question was not seriously addressed. No defense department ever owns up to its total ignorance on the subject and total indifference to the question.

The great contribution that cinematography and science fiction and cosmic theology can contribute to all of us is that they give us a language of "The End." A vocabulary to talk about "The End." Otherwise, we become like our bomb deciders who are speechless and voiceless about enduring values and access to vast hope. Apocalyptic stories keep us looking over the horizon.

The Book of Revelation presents a "what next" vision. This vision presumes a new, counterintuitive cosmic order. Instead of earth being "down here," and heaven being "up there," they would meld. Down would be up and up would be down. Heaven would no longer only be God's domain. Earth would no longer only be the domain of humans. Heaven would be the hidden dimension in ordinary life on earth, fully exposed.

Hints of this exist now, before the big bang at "The End." Hints of the operating principles at work when heaven and earth intersect. I saw this when I looked at nurses during the Covid-19 pandemic. I see it in folks who share their food. In children who embrace children unlike themselves. In those people who shelter the homeless and immigrants. In recovered addicts who give support to the addicted. This world is full of deep human caring and sacrifice that appears to reflect divine, otherworldly priorities. These folks seem more like angels from heaven. Their heavenly operating principles exist alongside the inherent human tendencies to dominate, profiteer, and exploit, as if nothing is sacred. Perhaps these exceptional people are previews of coming attractions, hints of what is coming when earth and heaven unite.

The biggest hope is that The End will obliterate the wall between earth and heaven and usher in a restored planet, a heaven-haunted planet, not a doomed wasteland. That would mean that when we die, we would not be a disembodied lot on our way up to an ethereal heaven. Instead, heaven itself, the new Jerusalem, would come down to claim all of us on earth. "God so loved the world!" (John 3:16) Earth and heaven would be merged, forever. Our life, our lives, all lives living and dead, would have standing and be terms of the merger.

That thinking was embedded from the beginning of the Bible. "Then the Lord formed man from the dust of the ground, and breathed into his nostrils the breath of life, and the man became a living being," (Genesis 2:7) From the beginning, our destiny was in the dust. Not transcendent but imminent. Incarnate. Tied to the fleshliness of all life. Forever, and not just during a span of life!

That thinking was embedded in the Lord's Prayer with the words, "Thy will be done on earth as it is in heaven." (Matthew 6:9-11) Thus, assuming that heaven is a "Nuclear Free Zone," we long for earth to emulate heaven.

As Henry David Thoreau wrote, "Heaven is under our feet as well as over our heads." Meanwhile, nukes are under our ground and flying overhead.

This apocalyptic high hope now resides in prayers, poetry and in the final vision of the Book of Revelation. But what would it take to make this merger operative? Answer: The end of all that we have known ... as well as the beginning of a domain that we can't truly imagine. We hope that the benign Spirit that created Earth in the beginning will brood over Earth's death at the end and ... have plans.

The first installment of this merger of earth and heaven, for me, took place in Jerusalem two thousand years ago when Jesus said, "All authority in heaven and earth has been given me." (Matthew 28:18) Dual citizenship, dual languages, dual destiny in one person! We got a glimpse of the new Jerusalem hanging from a tree in old Jerusalem. This was the picture of the end. When Jesus said, "It is finished," (John 19:30) I think that he was referring to the hold that evil has over the hearts and vanities of this world epitomized in a city.

Mythically, "it is finished" means that the ancient property dispute between the devil and God is determined in flesh and blood in Jerusalem. God's will is both defeated and triumphant there. Prophetically, "It is finished" means that, yes, there will be a day of reckoning with excruciating justice and that justice will be accompanied by the invisible, ineffable, crucified heart of God. Eschatologically, "It is finished" means that in Jerusalem a death is giving birth to the next iteration of life.

When Jesus said to the thief on the cross, "Today you will be with me in Paradise," (Luke 23:43) I think that the thief in old Jerusalem was to be the first citizen of the new Jerusalem.

WHAT DO YOU THINK? Do you think that lasting stability for this planet is possible in a nuclear-armed world? If so, what would that look like? If not, then what change in yourself and your government and all governments and all religions do you hope for so that all of us can survive in a nuclear-armed world?

CHAPTER 17

Beyond Hope

Dear George,

I believe that on August 6, 1945, human life on planet Earth was given an expiration date. Though Earth has been heated abnormally, cooled excruciatingly, polluted excessively, it has always, somehow, gotten by. Nevertheless, a star from afar might eat it, eventually. Or a meteor might denude it, in time. On the ground, artificial intelligence (AI) might find no good purpose for human life and thus dispose of it as time goes by. But now, now, now, nuclear weapons rest in the hands of severely flawed individuals and misguided regimes, guaranteeing that the day of finality is upon us. Yet, I believe that our demise will not be the last word.

A while ago I turned on the radio and heard an old man say, "I am ninety years old. Pretty soon now, I won't be here. And in a very little time after that, the people who know me will not be here either. And a little after that, there will not be one person on earth who ever knew me. Here is what my life is like: You get on a bus. You ride the bus. You get off the bus. And the bus goes on."

Certainly, that is true of the old man and me and everyone. But is it true of planet Earth? Will the time come when someone from another planet will peer through a telescope and see that life got off the bus here and the celestial transportation vehicle, Earth, moved on, riderless?

My heart thrills when I read in the Book of Revelation the part where it says, "He who was seated on the throne said, 'I make all things new … I am the Alpha and the Omega, the beginning and the end.'" The heart of those words reaches across the centuries and touches my heart. I lay aside for the moment all the complexities of that book's time-bound secret messages, and I take elaborate hope from the bold finality of the words "I make all things new."

Could the Author of Life produce life from atomic waste? And make all things new? What a breathtaking concept!

Yes, the James Webb Space Telescope is our latest word about life in the universe today. But there are other ways of seeing; other lenses through which to pick up signs of life. St. Paul once wrote, "For now we see through a glass darkly; but then face to face: now I know in part, but then I shall know even as also I am known." There might well be a dimension of knowing, of seeing that is as permanent, even more permanent, than witnessing black holes in space.

Just maybe the fate of the stars, planets, and life is not absolutely set in concrete. Behind the celestial order, perhaps there exists a regal realm of relationship—between the Divine and the human—that is characterized, at the least, by mercy, sacrifice, compassion, and co-creation. I do believe it exists and has staying power. Even we and our dying planet can be beneficiaries, even now.

The final question, perhaps, has to do with the mind of God. Or the Force. Or Creative Power. If God wills life for us creatures and all living beings, can that ultimate intent be thwarted? With our nuclear weapons? Even if life on earth ends? Can the will of the Originating Force be thwarted, in the end? Or is there no Originating Force, or one that cares about us?

Despite all evidence to the contrary, the biblical Job said, "I know that my Redeemer lives, and at the last, He will stand upon the earth." (Job 19:25-26) I don't get a vote on nuclear weapons, but I do have hope that the ending they occasion will not be the final word.

I do believe that we are "at the last." Which, with a resurrecting God, means that we are at the beginning. Maybe not today, but tomorrow or soon!

The atomic age is defined in terms of bombs. It started with a bomb and the age will end with bombs. Nothing human will follow this age. The story of the atomic age is a passion story. On YouTube, we can see the face of J. Robert Oppenheimer and hear his voice. All the lines in his face and all the heaviness in his voice betray the horror of what he had done and the dread that would inevitably follow. Passion in profile!

After Oppenheimer, we discovered in the words of Andrei Sakharov his deep sense of betrayal, his betrayal by arming short-term strategists with long-term consequences. Also, we saw his heroic efforts to limit the limitless damage that would certainly follow. Palpable passion!

Deep into the story of the bombs of the atomic age was the clear insight of Mikhail Gorbachev and Ronald Reagan. They sensed the heightened risk that the entire world was under through the out-of-control proliferation of bombs. So, they tiptoed to the edge of eliminating all the bombs, only to demur because of political pressures and their inability to make the final leap of trust. The haunting last moment missed and the guarantee of the passion story to come.

I hold up all the above against the passion story of Jesus. Passion because the entire enterprise was, for one crucial moment, out of his hands. Subsequently, surrendering his old life was required to find the path to the new life.

We are now living this passion story: life on planet Earth will be crucified on the cross of atomic darkness. Then a new day will dawn.

What do we do now, in the meantime? Answer: everything within our power to educate ourselves to the dangers, and to turn the public's attention to the apocalypse at hand, so that our societies might have one last chance to sustain human life on earth.

On the seventy-fifth Anniversary of the bombings of Hiroshima and Nagasaki, Voices for a World Free of Nuclear Weapons made a video called, "The Bomb: Past, Present and Future." For the script, I wrote:

> If you are young, demand urgent governmental action before these weapons rob you and your children of a future.
>
> If you are a diplomat, keep pounding away on the fulfillment of legal commitments already contained in treaties in force that call for the reduction and elimination of the threat posed by these weapons.
>
> If you are a religious leader, pray, preach, prophesy to stop the nuclear end of the world.
>
> If you are a politician, join parliamentarians and leaders world-wide who are working to stop the modernization and expansion of the capacity

of nuclear weapons in quality and quantity. And advance policies and legislation that reduce the threat of the use of the weapons, stop their spread, and lead to their elimination.

If you are a citizen, join a nuclear weapons abolition group, march in the streets, write letters, pray fervently, and demand that institutions stop investing in the nuclear weapons industry.

If you are a scientist, don't be used by politicians who champion nuclear stockpiles; instead, find solidarity in your ranks and reach across national boundaries to scientists in other nuclear-armed countries.

If you are an environmentalist, recognize that nuclear weapons are the immediate and ultimate climate change for all time; and

If you are a nation armed with nuclear weapons, join with other nuclear nations to establish a joint enterprise committed to working for the elimination of nuclear weapons.

We need to give birth to children who are not the targets of nuclear weapons.

If we refuse to be Earth's stewards, then there is a deeper ownership of Earth than the nuclear custodians of this moment. The rightful Author and Heir of Earth will, at last, claim and redeem it from the radioactive heap that will crown our atomic success and end the age of the human.

In the words of the poet John Donne as quoted by J. Robert Oppenheimer at the dawn of the atomic age, "So death doth touch Resurrection."

WHAT DO YOU THINK? Are we humans a rare exotic species which in time will become extinct, with no archival materials to prove that we existed? Do you have a "Beyond Hope" hope that sustains you in the atomic age? If so, what is it? Have you ever shared this hope with other people? Are you personally ready to do anything about the threat of nuclear weapons? If so, what? What do you think?

Postscript

George Shultz had everything to do with the genesis of this book and also with the genesis of Voices for a World Free of Nuclear Weapons (Voices), an organization that strives for global nuclear disarmament. I founded Voices after he asked me a question in 2007 that changed my life, and then he became the rock-solid undergirding of Voices, offering his considerable help.

So much vitality has burst forth from his sponsorship of Voices. First, Voices became an official Cooperation Circle of the United Religions Initiative, anchored in URI's Multi-Region.

Then George helped recruit some of his friends, including Dr. Sidney Drell, former Secretary of Defense William Perry, Ambassador Thomas Graham, Jr., and Ambassador James Goodby to join the group. In 2008 we began having monthly meetings, and these meetings have continued for over fifteen years—165 meetings and counting.

Eventually George assisted us in getting Mikhail Gorbachev to coordinate with Voices in inaugurating the annual Voices Youth Award. On December 13, 2020, on his one-hundredth birthday, George had the energy to perform one ceremony. He presented the First Annual Voices Youth Award, founded on his shared diplomatic legacy with Mikhail Gorbachev, to Kehkashan Basu of Toronto, Canada. In August 2023, we selected Yogev Von Kundra of southern Virginia to be the fourth annual recipient.

We Voices have tried to be opportunistic in addressing issues around disarmament. We have written op-eds, taken advocacy positions, spoken at conferences, and finally we have carved out our niche in the nuclear disarmament world. We centered on the spiritual, prayerful, and theological approaches to matters of nuclear weapons.

This approach started with a Nuclear Prayer of our own (see page 35), a prayer we have said at the beginning of our meetings for over twelve years. The same prayer! We made a very successful video of our members praying it together. This prayer has had a life of its own and has been said at the United Nations and around the world on numerous occasions. In 2022, we declared that August 6 would be the annual Nuclear Prayer Day for the entire world. Hundreds of thousands of people, globally, have written their own Nuclear Prayers. Our Third Annual Nuclear Prayer Day happens in 2024.

Voices has published remarkable newsletters, created an outstanding website (voices.uri.org), and developed a considerable media presence. Voices has produced a sixty-minute video of the seventy-fifth anniversary of the bombings of Hiroshima and Nagasaki and three educational videos on nuclear weapons for young children. We have made presentations at meetings of the Parliament of the World's Religions in Toronto and Chicago.

As part of the United Religions Initiative, Voices is the only large international interfaith group in the world that has been successful in getting all of the major international interfaith organizations to cooperate on a project, a filming project.

As of 2023, Voices has members from all parts of the United States and from India, Slovakia, Austria, and other countries.

All of this happened only because George and I became buddies when he married Charlotte.

Dear George,
Thank you for asking me what I thought.
Your friend,
Bill

Acknowledgements

Deserving of special praise for inspiring this book are the members of Voices for a World Free of Nuclear Weapons. Originally, former Secretary of State George Shultz, Dr. Sidney Drell, Ambassador Thomas Graham, Jr., Ambassador James Goodby, former Secretary of Defense William J. Perry, Monica Willard (United Religions Initiative delegate to the United Nations), and Jonathan Granoff.

We have been aided by outstanding Voices staff members including Julie Schelling, who made our newsletter a singular achievement, Haneen Khalid, Jenneth Macan Markar-Sonntag, and Katelynn Grace. These brilliant and overworked people took the expansive ideas about "what we should do next," and translated wild thinking into practical programs. Though not technically a staff member, Paul Andrews was fully engaged, making all the extra efforts successful.

For special projects, Audrey Kitagawa stands at the head of the class for her technical team's one-hour video. Also, the educational work of Carolyn MacKenzie, Vicki Garlock, and Dr. Charles Barker took us to a new dimension. Marilyn Turkovich did a stellar job of developing our Voices website. Linda Cataldo Modica and Michael Ramos doggedly kept our focus on matters of nuclear weapons at the most local levels. Barbara Newsom initiated new projects and did significant behind-the-scenes work.

Among our most steadfast members, in addition to those

just mentioned, have been Abraham Karickam in India, Keh-kashan Basu in Canada, Peter Rickwood in Austria, Mussie Hailu in Ethiopia, Isaac Thomas in Qatar, Mario Nicolini in Slovakia, Vincent Leong in Malaysia, Liliana Ashman, Anna Ikeda of Soka Gakkai International in Japan, and Carol Wolman, Diana Conan, Janessa Wilder, and Paul Chaffee in the United States.

Senator Sam Nunn offered his depth and experience when I needed assistance. Archbishop John Wester of the Archdiocese of New Mexico has been a brother in the struggle to rid the world of these weapons. Jonathan Granoff has been an inspiration to me because of his vast knowledge, indefatigable energy, and the capacious dimension of his soul. Monica Willard, who believed with all her heart in what we were doing, sparked almost every Voices effort.

Voices is a Cooperation Circle of the United Religions Initiative, an international interfaith organization. I would like to thank other international interfaith organizations that have partnered at times with Voices: Religions for Peace, Charter for Compassion, and the Parliament of the World's Religions. Also, a major collaborator with Voices has been the Japanese Buddhist organization, Soka Gakkai International.

John Weiser has been a close and attentive friend through all my writings, workings, projects, and meetings and has partnered with me to finish this book.

Several people worked to turn the manuscript for *God and Nuclear Weapons* into book form. When my computer caused me tribulation, it was our granddaughter, Julia Swing, who brought order out of my chaos. Editor Sally W. Smith offered an insightful and inspiring critique of the manuscript. Then the publishing team of Sandra Gary, Maureen Perry, and Barbara Geisler conjured their magic. At the last minute, cartoonist Signe Wilkinson came to my rescue.

Finally, I would like to celebrate the memory of the late William K. Bowes, Jr., who gave me the money to make most of the work of Voices possible.

As the reader can see, many inspired people influenced this book. I thank them all with all my heart.

Made in the USA
Las Vegas, NV
15 October 2024